BIG AND Little

ACTIVITY DEVOTIONAL

Printed in the United States of America

978-1-5359-5925-4

Published by B&H Publishing Group
Nashville, Tennessee

Design and illustration by Jacy Corral.

1 2 3 4 5 6 7 • 24 23 22 21 20

BIG AND Little
ACTIVITY DEVOTIONAL
Go to NINEVEH!
B&H
BHPUBLISHING.COM
B&H PUBLISHING
NASHVILLE, TENNESSEE
WRITTEN BY RACHEL C. SWANSON & ILLUSTRATED BY JACY CORRAL

Hi Friend!

While there's no right or wrong way to use this book, let us help give you a starting point on how best to utilize it.

1. You will notice the pages are laid out opposite facing. This is to encourage eye contact and conversation with the child in front of you.
2. If the child can read, have them read aloud the verse or passage of Scripture on their page. If not, please read it out loud together.
3. Then, read out loud the devotional which gives a summary of the story and key point.
4. Ask the "For Kids…" question to the child and listen for their response.
5. Ask the "For Grown Ups..." question to yourself and ponder on it.
6. Enjoy working on your activities, together!

This book is designed so you can both connect at the same time using your heart, head, and hands as you learn about the biblical stories and key points from those stories. There is an answer key at the back of the book as well in case you get stuck.

It's an honor and joy to bring this Big and Little Activity Devotional to you and those you share it with. Share with other by using the hashtag #bigandlittleactivitydevotional online!

With Joy,
Jacy Corral and Rachel C. Swanson

Help Jonah Get to Nineveh

The word of the LORD came to Jonah son of Amittai: "Get up! Go to the great city of Nineveh and preach against it because their evil has come up before me." Jonah got up to flee to Tarshish from the LORD's presence. He went down to Joppa and found a ship going to Tarshish. He paid the fare and went down into it to go with them to Tarshish from the LORD's presence. *(Jonah 1:1–3)*

Solution on page 73

Solve the Maze

For Kids...
How will God respond to you when you come to Him with a repentant heart? What's one thing you've done that you need to ask God's forgiveness for?

Jonah ran away from God's command for him to preach the gospel in Nineveh. After fleeing on a ship, encountering a massive storm, and getting swallowed by a great fish (also known as a whale) for three days, Jonah finally came to God with a repentant heart, accepting his assignment and was expelled from the fishes mouth! This time when he was commanded again to go, Jonah went to the city, sharing the gospel message to the king and all the people there and because he was faithful, these people repented of their evil ways. (Go to Jonah chapters 1–3 for the entire story!)

For Grown Ups...
Don't be afraid to demonstrate repentance in front of your children by saying you're sorry when you make a mistake (ie., showing anger in front of them) and then enter into a time of repentant prayer to Jesus with them.

Solution on page 73

How many can you find and color?

_______ fish

_______ loaves of bread

_______ baskets

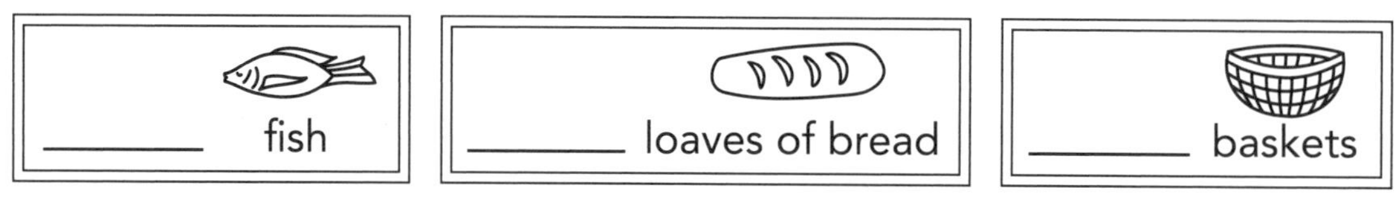

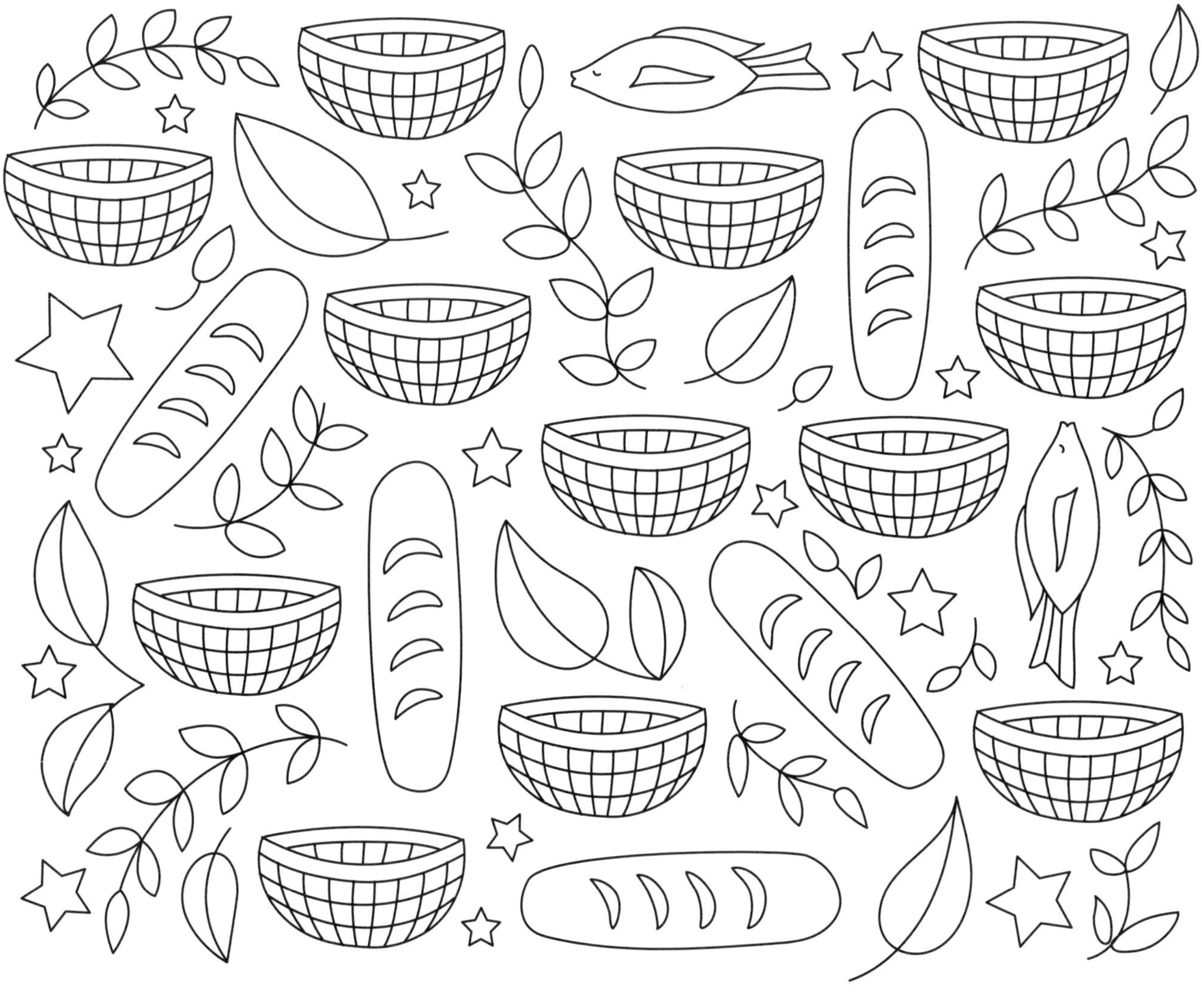

"But we only have five loaves and two fish here," they said to him. "Bring them here to me," he said. Then he commanded the crowds to sit down on the grass. He took the five loaves and the two fish, and looking up to heaven, he blessed them. He broke the loaves and gave them to the disciples, and the disciples gave them to the crowds. Everyone ate and was satisfied. They picked up twelve baskets full of leftover pieces. Now those who ate were about five thousand men, besides women and children. *(Matthew 14:17–21)*

Solution on page 73

		4			2	5	9	1
		6	3	1				
						7		
	8	9	2	6				
	5		7	4	3		8	
			9	5		1	3	
		3						
				8	7	3		
1	7	8	5			2		

Jesus went away from the villages to rest, but the crowds followed Him, so He continued teaching the people about God. Hours passed, and the people grew hungry but realized they had nothing to eat. The disciples asked around for food and a small boy gave them five loaves of bread and two fish. Jesus blessed the bread and fish, thanking God for this provision and passed the basket around to everyone. The food multiplied and more than five thousand men, women, and children ate their fill! In fact, there was plenty of food leftover! Another demonstration of God's faithfulness and provision!

For Kids...
In what ways has God provided for you? What has this done to your faith in Him?

For Grown Ups...
With your child, write down a list of things God has provided to you. Practice this heart of thankfulness, remembering the things God has provided and thank Him for all the blessings—big and small—that He gives.

Solution on page 74

Lost and Found Word Search

Search for the words in the key.

N	T	A	R	I	N	B	O	L	A
I	E	L	O	S	T	A	U	G	W
M	A	M	X	E	E	P	L	E	S
R	L	S	G	H	A	F	V	E	N
A	T	C	A	R	N	O	P	L	I
O	L	Y	W	E	L	U	A	Y	P
J	R	P	A	P	O	N	V	Q	E
R	J	S	O	A	Z	D	M	P	E
S	O	R	T	W	I	E	M	O	H
E	Y	C	M	E	L	R	S	I	S

LOST FOUND JOY LOVE SHEEP

So he told them this parable: "What man among you, who has a hundred sheep and loses one of them, does not leave the ninety-nine in the open field and go after the lost one until he finds it? When he has found it, he joyfully puts it on his shoulders, and coming home, he calls his friends and neighbors together, saying to them, 'Rejoice with me, because I have found my lost sheep!'" *(Luke 15:3–6)*

Solution on page 74

Luke 15 Word Search

```
L D W A S N G R O W E S A C V M S L E Y T G U I N
A T E P N E I G H B O R U I P Q U J S G P O E W T
W C O M G P H R A M G I Q T S V P K X O R N F H G
G Y P T E L Q F H L F G W A L A U R L E S T L I O
L I H G P F U M P D U H M O W H G T P I X A G H Q
R E J O I C E C U A P T I H A S D E A O L I J U D
A W P R A B J X T I Y E S K U I N A S P T G Q P S
Y G T Q Y G O G Y A P O B V L T U F T N F K S O U
M L I U F T L H P G R U Y C A B Q H U A W H F T N
Y R E P G O M U A E M S X N P R O M R J X C S E G
Q L X I T W J G I U L N C D S Z W K E K R I O H L
U Y R E O U A E V A T E B Y A D P S D T F G B I E
Q D C N G N Y K L O E S P I L Q H T B N W E A L J
I O P L E Z C P D G I S J A S U Y D K G L U K E K
B M K S T M G O A Q W Y L Z M J E C D Y T W J U H
N I R M H Y I K E R J O K Q A P S T O X N L A P O
O C Q Y E W G N S T A P I P E T D A P I B H K I M
X E U V R S D P C W E B N G W O H R E F O A G X E
S T I B W L J O F D U R L F B U I S D C L I R T W
P Q L K A T G Y I R Z O K E D S H E P H E R D F G
```

HOME
LUKE
NEIGHBOR
PARABLE
PASTURE
REJOICE
REPENTANCE
RIGHTEOUSNESS
SHEPHERD
TOGETHER

Jesus loved to tell stories. One day He asked, "What would happen if you had one hundred sheep and one got lost? What would you do? Wouldn't you leave the ninety-nine and go looking for the one? After finding the lost sheep, wouldn't it be appropriate to joyfully share this news with others?" This is what God does. He never stops pursuing the one who goes astray, and God celebrates when those who go astray return to Him.

For Kids...

Have you ever gone the wrong way or been lost before? When we make bad choices like lying, cheating, or being unkind to others, we are going astray from God. What bad choices have you made that you need to ask for God's forgiveness? Remember, He will always accept you back with open arms.

For Grown Ups...

Have you ever lost something near and dear to you, but found it again? Halleluiah, right? Dwell on how this made you feel and remember that this is how God feels about you, times infinity, when you turn your heart back to Him.

Solution on page 74

Connect the Dots to Help Noah Build the Arc

"'Make yourself an ark of gopher wood. Make rooms in the ark, and cover it with pitch inside and outside.' And Noah did this. He did everything that God had commanded him." *(Genesis 6:14, 22)*

Connect the Dots and Trace the Dashed Lines

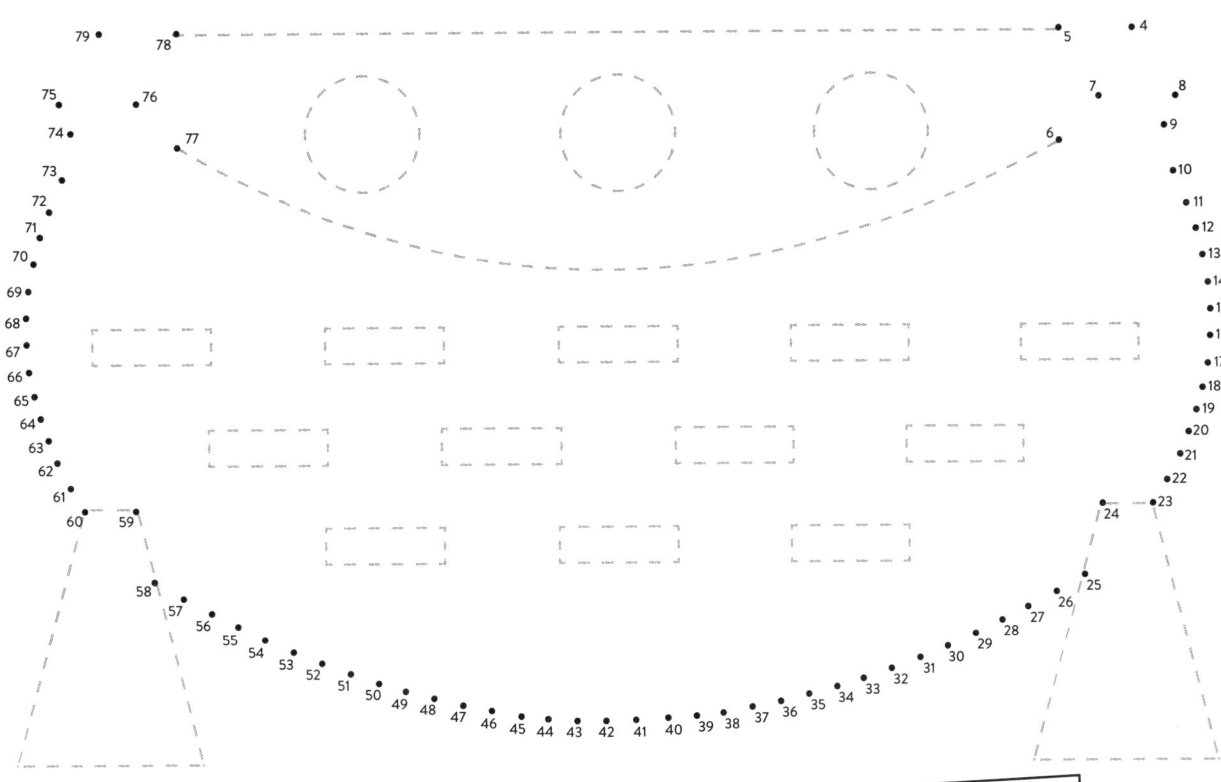

Picture for a moment being Noah. You were just told by God to create this massive boat, an undertaking like none other for this day and time, without all the gadgets and materials that we have today. Would you automatically and enthusiastically say "Yes!"? Truthfully, I sit back in awe, admiring Noah's quick and steady obedience and commitment to completing this task. It was not only really difficult but took decades to complete. Are you as quick to say, "Yes" to God's commands? Obeying isn't just through words but is followed by actions.

For Kids...

Obeying means doing what you're asked. Are you quick to obey your parents when they ask you to clean your room, make your bed, or brush your teeth? Remember, obeying is meant to help you become responsible, and it demonstrates love to your parents through your obedience. In the same way, how can we show our love for God?

For Grown Ups...

Obeying God's biblical commandments to love others, bestow kindness, not steal, not covet and more, are encouraged from a high and mighty God, but it's the way we demonstrate our love for God and enjoy the fruits of being obedient. How can you create a positive change to correcting a less-than-fruitful habit in your life?

Follow the Numbers to Color the Sun

In the beginning God created the heavens and the earth...God saw all that He had made, and it was all very good indeed. *(Genesis 1:1, 31)*

Color by Numbers

1 - Red
2 - Orange
3 - Yellow

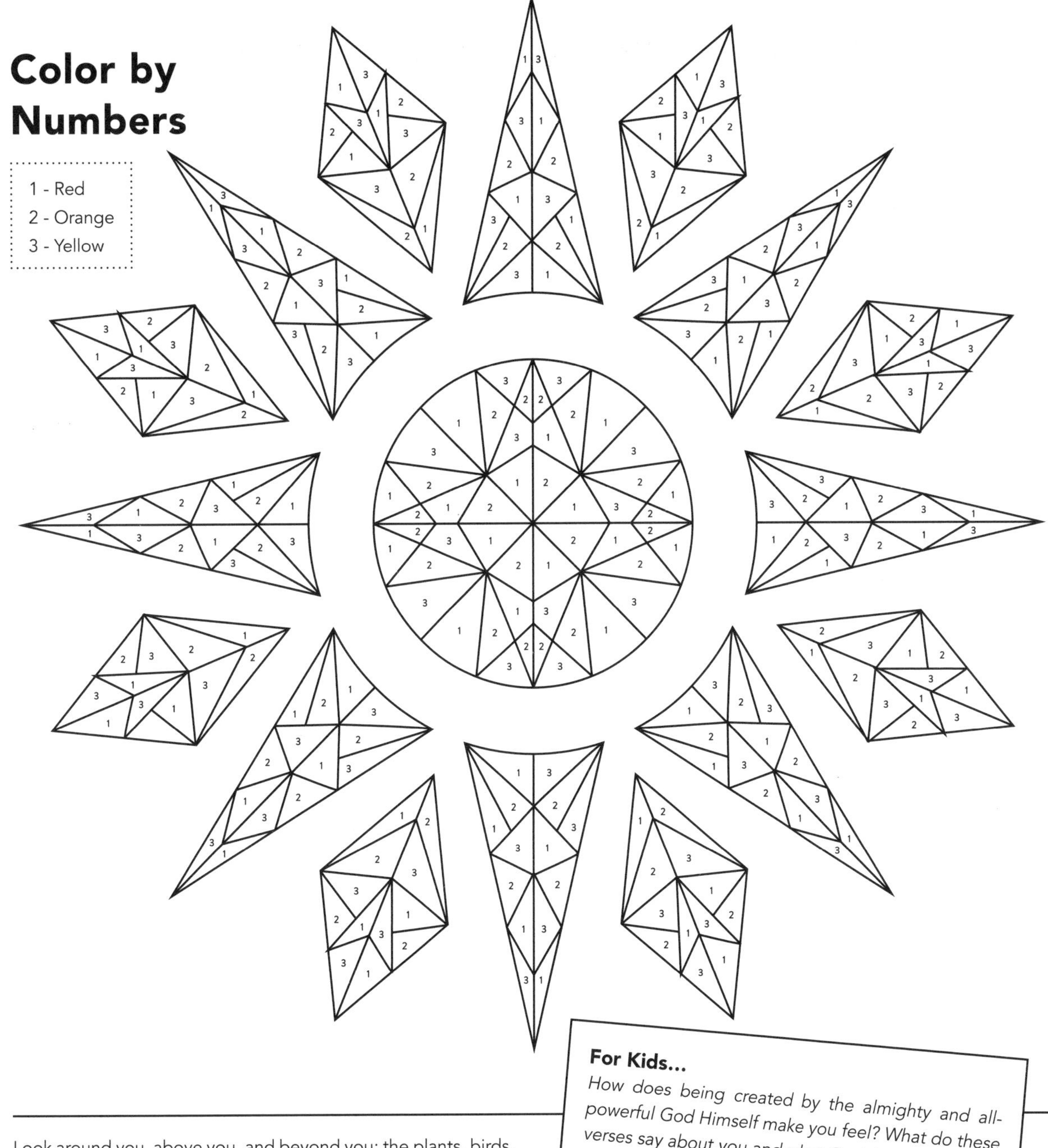

For Kids...
How does being created by the almighty and all-powerful God Himself make you feel? What do these verses say about you and what God thinks of you?

Look around you, above you, and beyond you: the plants, birds, sun, stars, and even the person right in front of you was created by God. And God says everything He made was very good, indeed. In fact, I believe God saved the best for last—creating us in His image! What an incredible thing to be created in the likeness of God! We were created on purpose for a purpose and "God don't make no junk." Don't forget the awe and wonder of just being you.

For Grown Ups...
Often, we forget how special we truly are and have lost the awe of being created in the image of God. Do you know how special you are? Don't forget your identity comes from being a child of God and that's worth more than any title of this world.

Follow the Steps to Draw a Crown

Step 1: Use a pencil to draw a rectangle with a zig zag top.

Step 2: Add diamonds between each zig zag with small diamonds and circles in between each one.

Step 3: Draw smaller diamonds inside the large ones. Add a row of circles on the bottom and erase the straight line.

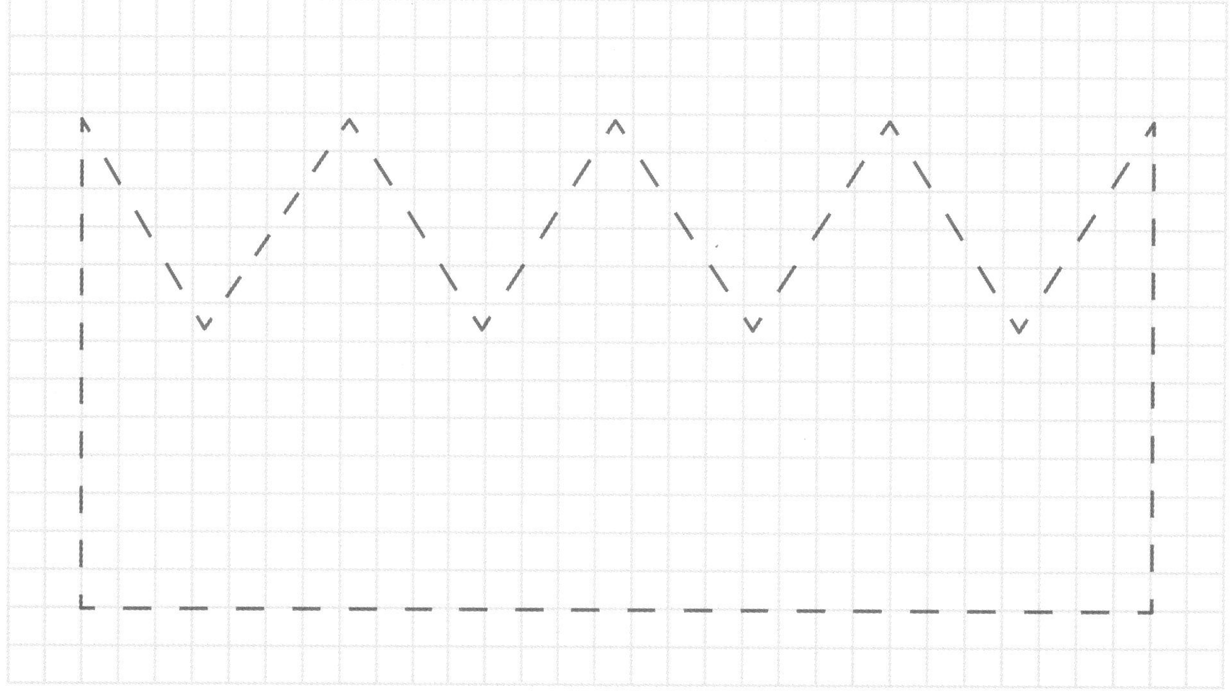

Mordecai told the messenger to reply to Esther..."Who knows, perhaps you have come to your royal position for such a time as this."...Esther sent this reply to Mordecai: "Go and assemble all the Jews who can be found in Susa and fast for me. Don't eat or drink for three days, night or day. I and my female servants will also fast in the same way." *(Esther 4:13a–16)*

Follow the Steps to Draw a Crown

Step 1: Draw two ellipses with a zig zag top.

Step 2: Erase the center third from the bottom and connect. Add circles to the peak of each zig zag, and gem shapes inside.

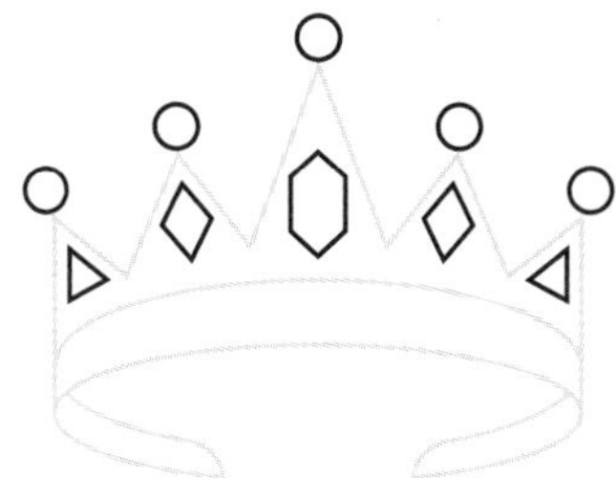

Step 3: Add smaller cirlces inside each circle, matching shapes inside each gem, and detail lines. Add tear drop shapes between the gems.

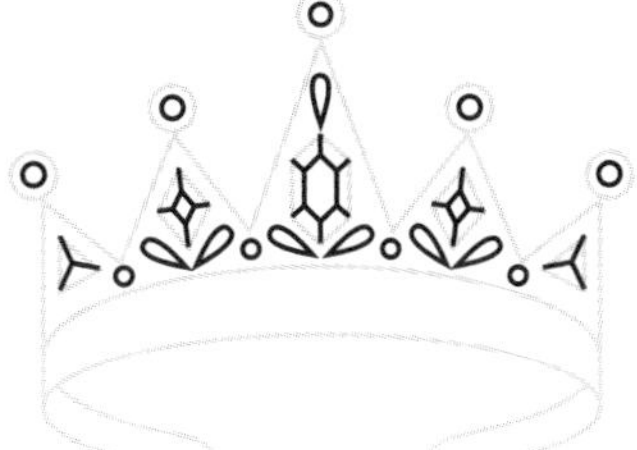

Step 4: Add semetrical florish lines to the band.

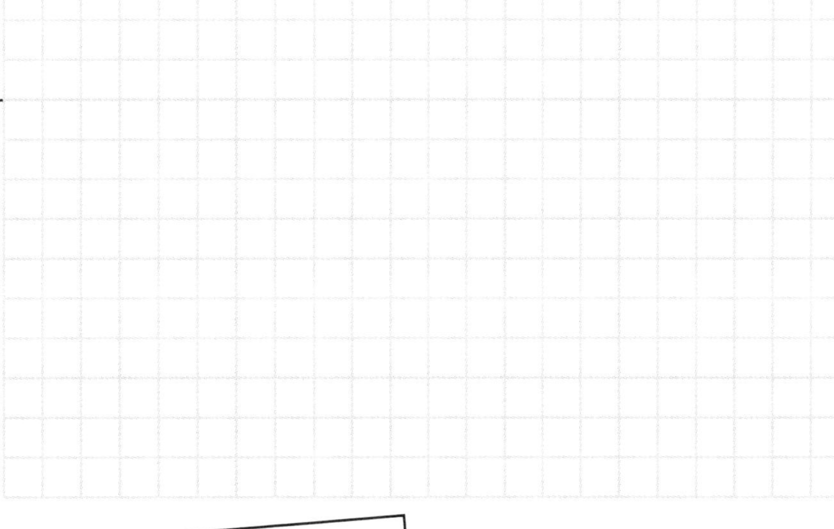

Esther was a simple girl, raised in a simple family. She was a Jew living in a kingdom overtaken by a Persian King. One day, God flipped her world upside down, and she became the Queen of all of Persia! The Kingdom didn't know she was Jewish, until one day she was forced to make the decision to reveal her heritage because of an evil plan a man named Haman; who was plotting to destroy all the Jews in the land. She was afraid, because to go before the King with a request, even as the Queen, could put her life in danger. Mordecai, her Jewish cousin, encouraged her to see her situation with a new lens: that she was placed in this position for a key purpose to save her people. Ultimately, the schemes by Haman were revealed to the King and her people were saved. Her courage, willingness to seek God through prayer and fasting, and waiting on His timing were key to solving this issue.

For Kids...
There's a reason you have been placed in your classroom, or soccer team, even family for such a time as this. Who needs help around you? What task has God positioned you to complete right now?

For Grown Ups...
You too have been placed where you are for "such a time as this." Is there a coworker God wants you to love? Do you have certain responsibilities at church or at home that need your specific skills, giftings, or insights? Don't forget that you've been placed where you are on purpose for a purpose.

Decode the Verse

Match each shape to the word in the key.

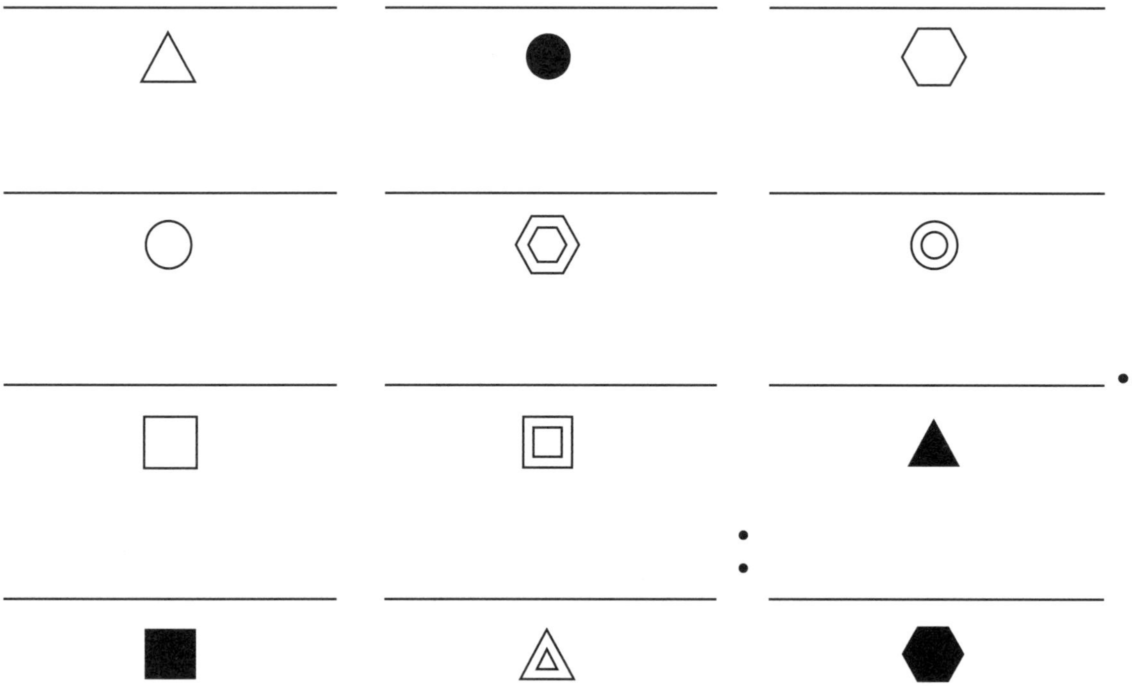

______	______	______
△	●	⬡
______	______	______
○	⬡ (double)	◎
______	______	______ .
□	▣	▲
______	______ :	______
■	△ (double)	⬢

○	AHEAD	▲	LIFE	□	TO
■	GENESIS	⬡	ME	◎	YOU
△	GOD	▣	PRESERVE	⬢	5
⬡ (double)	OF	●	SENT	△ (double)	45

"I am Joseph, your brother," he said, "the one you sold into Egypt. And now don't be grieved or angry with yourselves for selling me here, because God sent me ahead of you to preserve life." (*Genesis 45:4–5*)

Solution on page 75

Fill in the letters that correspond to the numbers below the blanks to solve the phrase.

A	B	C	D	E	F	G	H	I	J	K	L	M	N	O	P	Q	R	S	T	U	V	W	X	Y	Z
23	22					5			9								3								

" _/13 A/23 _/11 J/9 _/16 _/4 _/6 _/18 _/8 , _/7 _/16 _/24 R/3 B/22 R/3 _/16 _/19 _/8 _/6 R/3 " , _/8 _/6

_/4 A/23 _/13 _/10 , " _/19 _/8 _/6 _/16 _/20 _/6 _/7 _/16 _/24 _/4 _/16 _/21 _/10 _/13 _/20 _/19 _/16

_/6 G/5 _/7 _/18 _/19 . A/23 _/20 _/10 _/20 _/16 _/2 _/10 _/16 _/20 ' _/19 B/22 _/6 G/5 R/3 _/13 _/6 _/16 _/6 _/10

_/16 R/3 A/23 _/20 G/5 R/3 _/7 _/2 _/13 _/19 _/8 _/7 _/16 _/24 R/3 _/4 _/6 _/21 _/26 _/6 _/4 _/12 _/16 R/3

_/4 _/6 _/21 _/21 _/13 _/20 G/5 _/11 _/6 _/8 _/6 R/3 _/6 , B/22 _/6 _/25 A/23 _/24 _/4 _/6 G/5 _/16 _/10

_/4 _/6 _/20 _/19 _/11 _/6 A/23 _/8 _/6 A/23 _/10 _/16 _/12 _/7 _/16 _/24 _/19 _/16

_/18 R/3 _/6 _/4 _/6 R/3 _/26 _/6 _/21 _/13 _/12 _/6 . " G/5 _/6 _/20 _/6 _/4 _/13 _/4 45 : 4 - 5

When Joseph was a young man, he had a dream (from God) that he would rule over his brothers and family. It wasn't the kind of dream you would want to tell family, especially when your brothers already hated you. Honestly, it probably sounded like he was just being pride. Over the next twelve years of Joseph's life, instead of seeing this dream come true, he was beaten, tossed in a ditch by his brothers, sold as a slave, and thrown in jail for wrongdoings he never committed. Would this dream ever come true? Eventually, it did. God positioned him through a series of events to become second in command next to Pharaoh, helping Joseph save the people of Egypt from a harsh famine he predicted (through God) would take place. Years later, when his brothers approached Joseph (whom they didn't recognize at first) for help from the famine, instead of telling them "I told you so" with arrogance, he welcomed them, extending grace and forgiveness to his brothers, demonstrating growth in his character. God brought Joseph on a journey toward humility through difficulty, but it was worth it in the end.

For Kids...

Do you brag about your accomplishments in front of other kids your age? This can bring jealousy and envy by others. Next time when you find the urge to boast, ask yourself, "Does sharing this information provide value to others or encourage them?" If not, it may be wiser to keep those thoughts to yourself or simply share them with God instead!

For Grown Ups...

C. S. Lewis states "Humility is not thinking less of yourself but thinking of yourself less." Is there an area in your life—marriage, parenting, or work—that God may be allowing difficulty for you to learn deeper humility?

Solution on page 75

Color the Sword and Shield

The LORD said to Gideon, "You have too many troops for me to hand the Midianites over to them, or else Israel might elevate themselves over me and say, 'My own strength saved me.' Now announce to the troops: 'Whoever is fearful and trembling may turn back and leave Mount Gilead.' *(Judges 7:2–3)*

Trace and Color the Sword and Shield

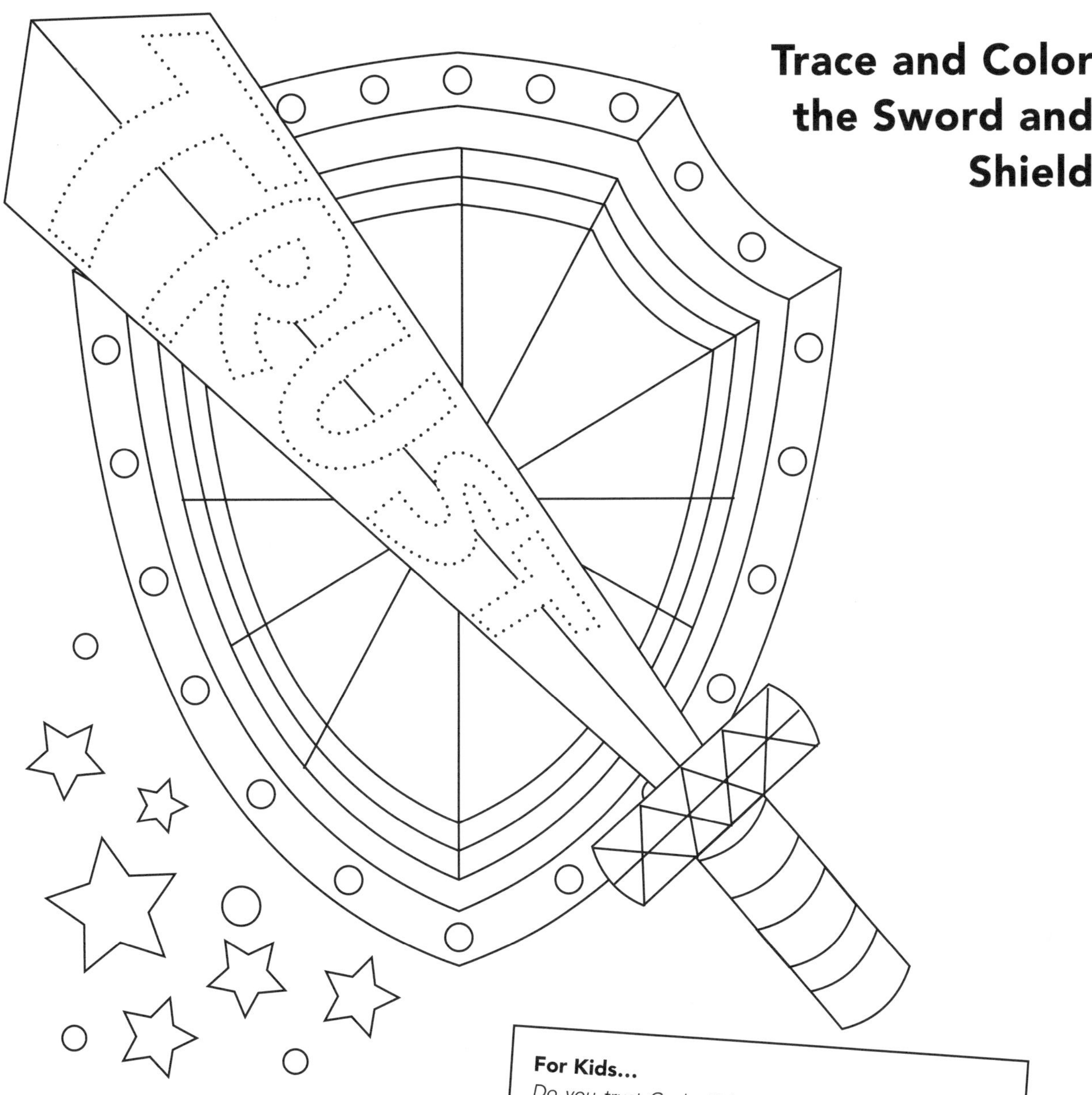

For Kids...

Do you trust God will help you when you face a tricky situation? The Bible says those who know Jesus can trust in Him (Ps. 9:10). He won't ever leave you and will help you in every situation.

For Grown Ups...

Are you trusting God with your finances, relationships, or other areas of your life that feel hard? Are you mustering things in your own strength? Remember, God is with you. He is ready to help you. He can be trusted because He loves you more than you will ever know.

The story of Gideon is a story about trust. God kept asking Gideon to lower the number of men in his army used against the Midianite army of the land. This doesn't seem to make sense. Normally, the larger the army, the more likely success would come. Ultimately, God wanted to demonstrate His strength over human strength to defeat the army, overcoming this battle not by sheer numbers but through the strength and power of God. Gideon trusted God, followed His plan, and defeated the Midianite army against all odds.

Search and Find the Following Items in the Picture

Paintbrush Wheat Stalk Heart Caterpillar Envelope

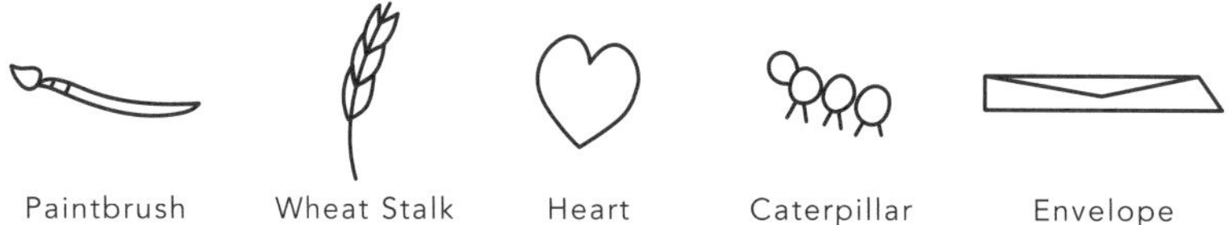

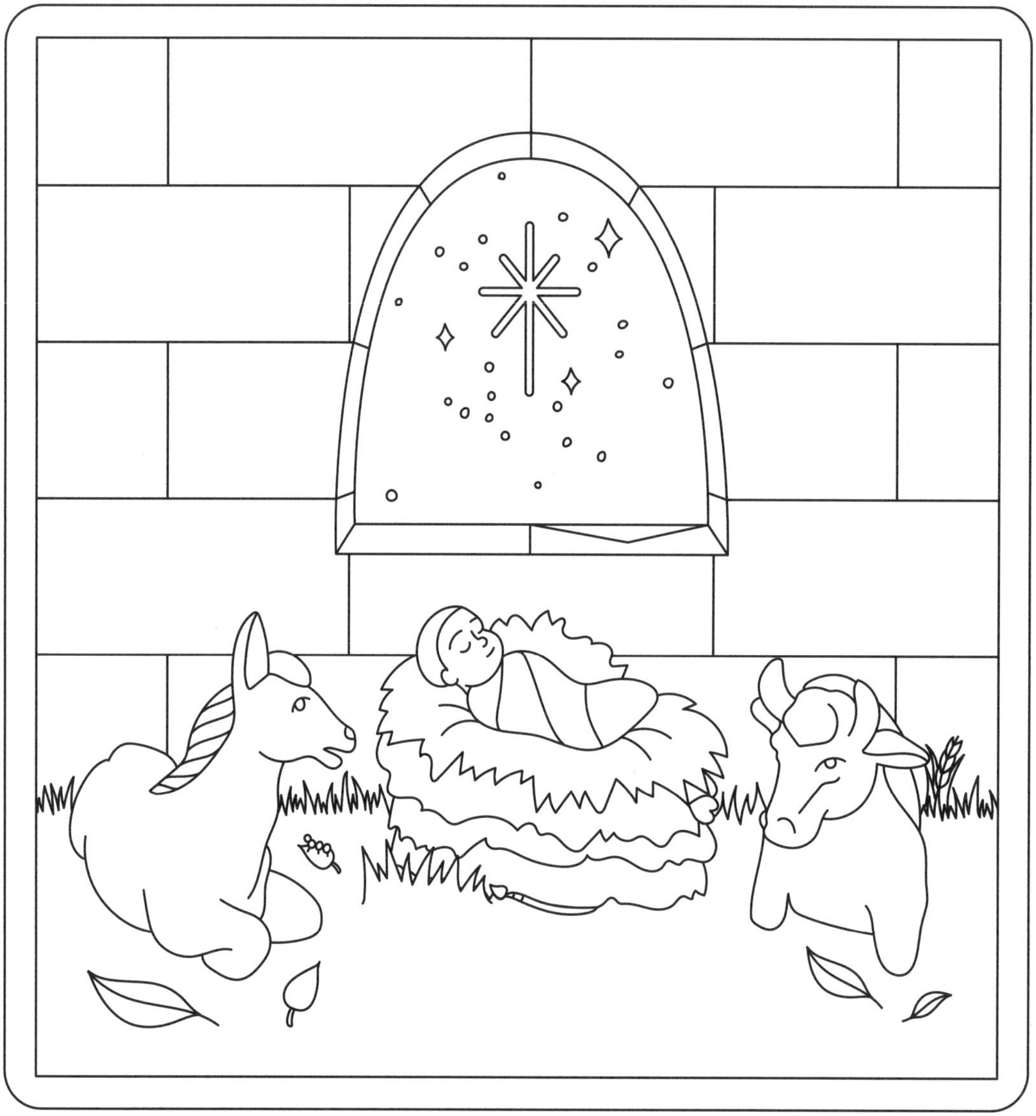

Then she gave birth to her firstborn son [Jesus], and she wrapped him tightly in cloth and laid him in a manger, because there was no guest room available for them. (*Luke 2:7*)

Solution on page 76

Search and Find

Don't you find it fitting that the King of the universe entered the world through a baby? Mary and Joseph were simple people, and instead of a grand palace, or even a decent home to birth Jesus—our heavenly King—in, she was forced to have him in a random stable filled with cows, sheep, and horses. Not only that, the king of Kings was born in a manger—a feeding trough for animals—filled with hay. What a demonstration that makes us special doesn't come from our surroundings, but, simply, from being a child of God. Just as God had a distinct and beautiful purpose for Jesus, He has a distinct and beautiful purpose for you, too, that moves beyond your surroundings.

For Kids...
What does this say about where your significance and purpose come from? What does this say about the kid struggling across town? Where does his or her purpose come from?

For Grown Ups...
Where do you find your purpose? In your titles, achievements, surroundings? Or is it found in the deeper part of who you really are—a child of God—that can't be taken away? Reflect on this right now.

Solution on page 76

Matthew 4 Crossword

Read the verses at the bottom of the page for clues.

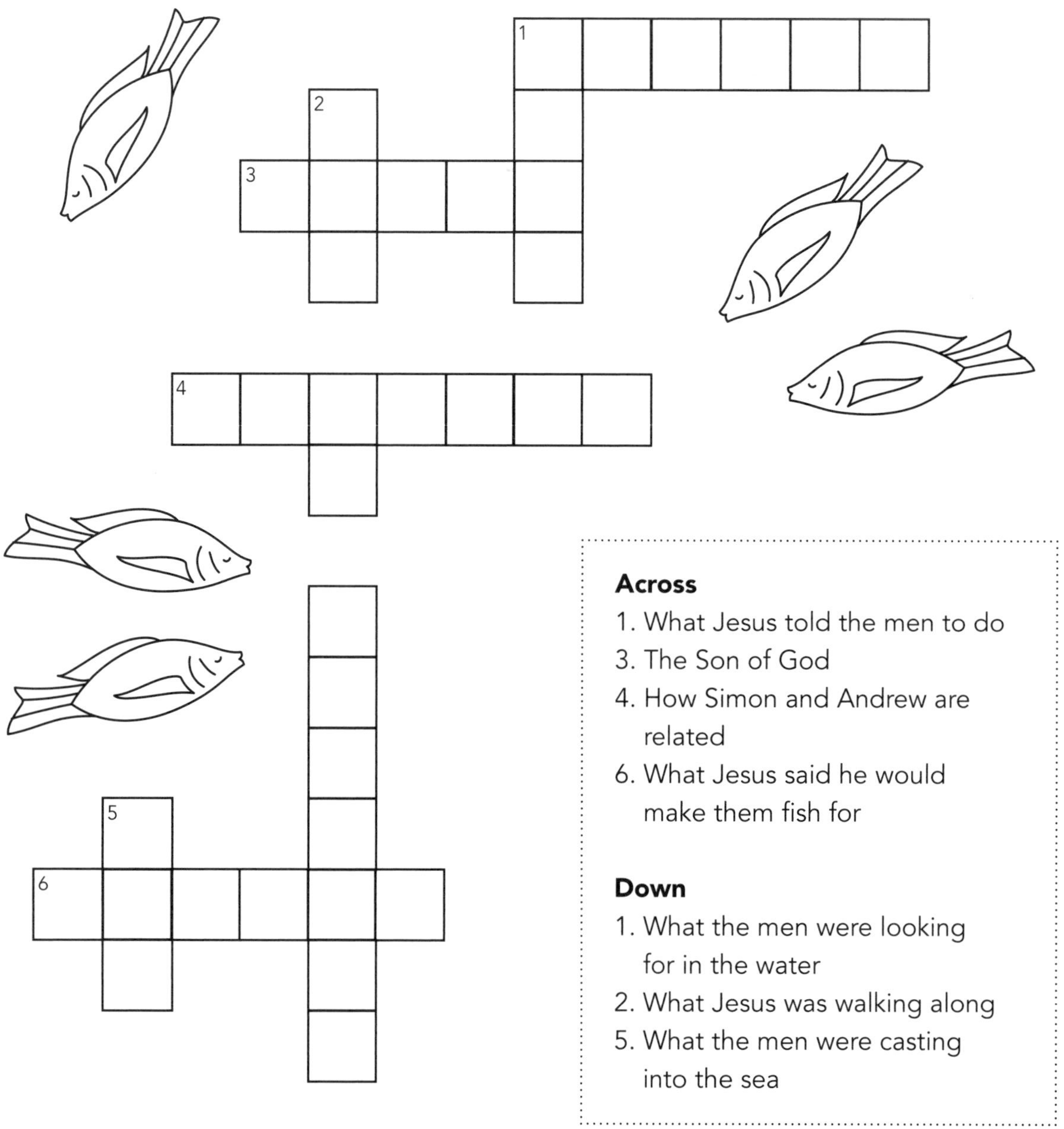

Across

1. What Jesus told the men to do
3. The Son of God
4. How Simon and Andrew are related
6. What Jesus said he would make them fish for

Down

1. What the men were looking for in the water
2. What Jesus was walking along
5. What the men were casting into the sea

As he was walking along the Sea of Galilee, he saw two brothers, Simon (who is called Peter), and his brother Andrew. They were casting a net into the sea—for they were fishermen. "Follow me," he told them, "and I will make you fish for people." Immediately they left their nets and followed him. *(Matthew 4:18–20)*

Solution on page 76

Matthew 4 Crossword

Across

3. Used to catch fish
4. The Son of God
6. A structure that support vines
10. Humans
11. Ancestry
12. A course of action
13. Ruler
14. A follower of Jesus
16. Feeling fear
18. To involve oneself
19. The Word of God
21. The first gospel
22. Peter's old name
23. Driving surface
25. The occupation of the brothers
27. A large body of water
28. To proceed
29. Peter's brother
30. To refuse or oppose
31. The name of God
33. The study of the past

Down

1. Arched area of the human foot
2. To go after
5. To aid the interests of
7. Grouping
8. Urges on
9. Males
15. The legal right to another's property until a debt is paid
17. A request for someone's participation
20. Without delay
24. Journeys
26. To surround on all sides
28. A means of access
32. Demonstrate
34. Proclaim

For Kids...

Have you shared the love of Jesus with a friend yet? I encourage you to find one person this week, who doesn't know about Jesus, and tell them how much He loves them too.

Can you imagine dropping everything—your career, your stuff, your community—and following an unknown path and plan? Peter and Andrew were successful fishermen. Suddenly, they were invited to not just sit on the sidelines, watching all that Jesus was doing, but they were invited to share the gospel message with Him. It's one thing to sit and listen to the truth, without action. It's another to actively live out what you believe to be true.

For Grown Ups...

Do you actively share about the love of Jesus and what He's done for your life? What if instead of reading about people of the Bible sharing the gospel with others, we actually shared the gospel message with others about God's love and sacrifice too? Think of one person you can share with this week and put it on your calendar to reach out so you don't forget.

Solution on page 77

Joshua 6:1-5 Maze

First draw seven circles around the city. Then, start at the center to solve the maze!

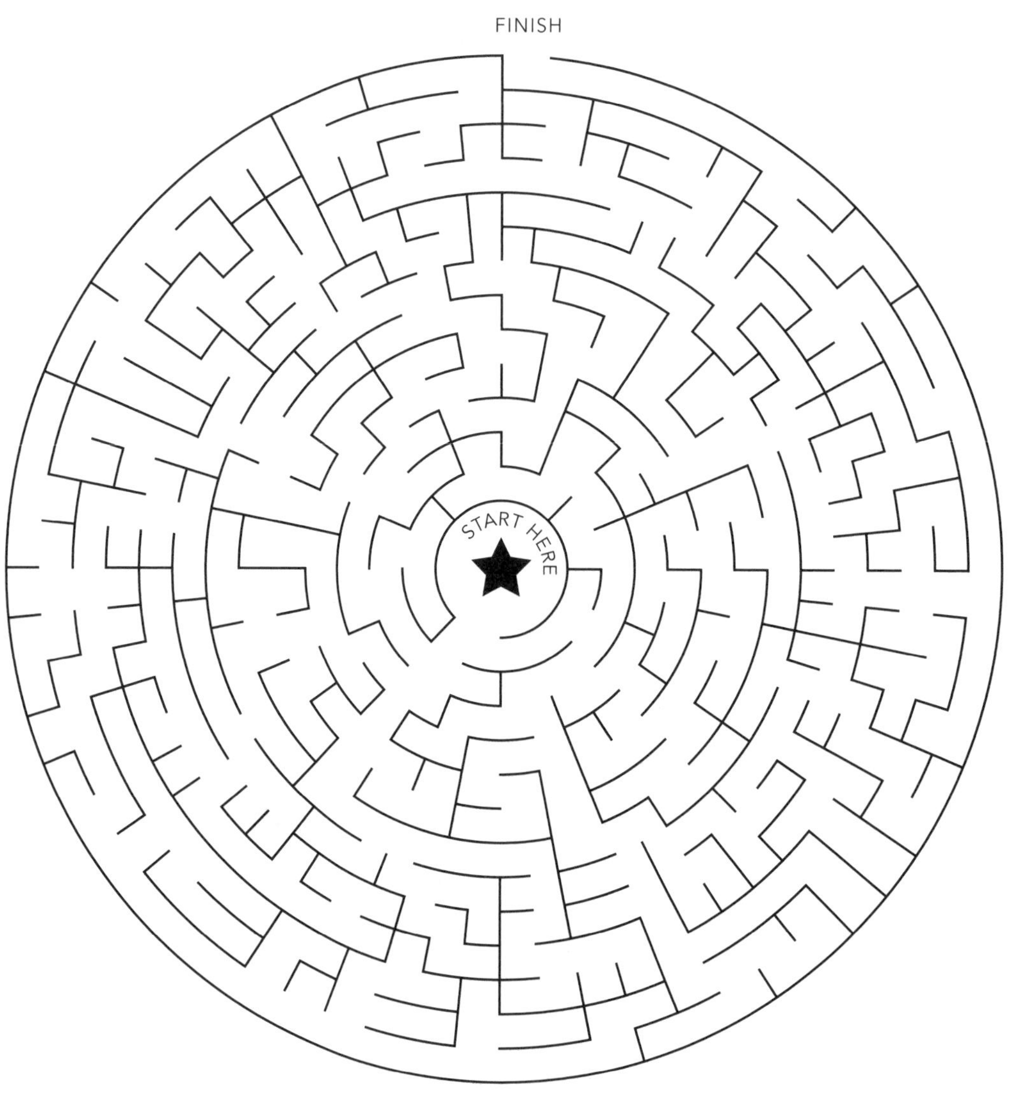

The LORD said to Joshua... "March around the city with all the men of war, circling the city one time. Do this for six days. Have seven priests carry seven ram's-horn trumpets in front of the ark. But on the seventh day, march around the city seven times, while the priests blow the trumpets. When there is a prolonged blast of the horn and you hear its sound, have all the troops give a mighty shout. Then the city wall will collapse, and the troops will advance, each man straight ahead." *(Joshua 6:1–5)*

Solution on page 77

Solve the Maze

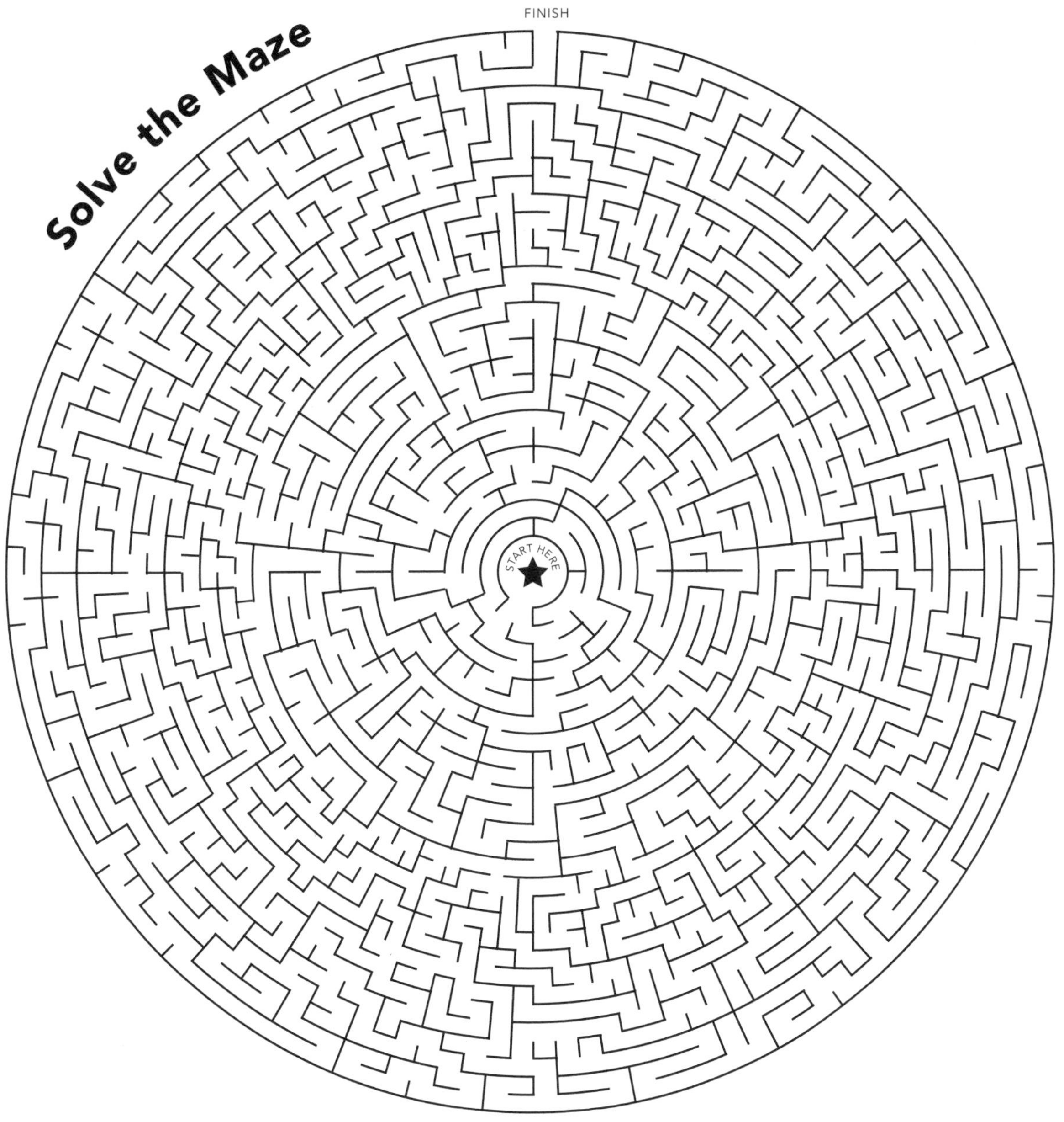

Can you imagine being told by God to do this? I mean, it doesn't make sense to think that circling around the city walls every day for six days, then marching around seven times on the seventh day, tooting horns and shouting would make stone walls come down. But that's exactly what Joshua and his tribe did, faithfully believing God would come through on His promise. We can trust God, even when it doesn't seem to make sense. God doesn't hold out on us or His promises for us.

For Kids...
Do you know what God's promises are to you? Have someone read to you 1 John 1:8–9 (God will always forgive), Jeremiah 29:11 (God is always working for your good), 1 Corinthians 10:13 (God will always give you a way out).

For Grown Ups...
Reflect on the above promises that God gives to you.

Solution on page 77

Color the Verse

"You are the light of the world. A city situated on a hill cannot be hidden. No one lights a lamp and puts it under a basket, but rather on a lampstand, and it gives light for all who are in the house. In the same way, let your light shine before others, so that they may see your good works and give glory to your Father in heaven." *(Matthew 5:14–16)*

Trace and Color the Verse

Have you ever been on an airplane at night and looked down at the cities below? The lights sparkle and light up the night sky, each one penetrating the darkness with light. Each one of you adds light to this world when you do good works, giving glory to God. Others see this light shining out from within, noticing something different from the the rest of the world. You are meant to stand out and shine. Don't be afraid to shine so others can see God's love in you.

For Kids...
Think about all the ways that you can shine for Jesus? (Through kind words, thoughtful actions, or respectful approaches.) What is something that you can do today that will add light and love to the life of one of your friends or family members?

For Grown Ups...
Is your spiritual life a bit dull and dim? When our hearts and minds aren't activated by God, our light begins to fade. So, start simple. Send a text to a friend letting them know you're thinking of them. Take a gift to a neighbor. Write a love note to your spouse. Fill up your own light inside of you by reading God's Word every day.

Mark 12:30 Word Scramble

Unscramble each word. Use the verse at the bottom of the page for clues!

ELVO ____________________

REHAT ____________________

LUSO ____________________

RNESTTGH ____________________

IMND ____________________

OEINGBRH ____________________

SFYEURLO ____________________

KARM ____________________

"Love the Lord your God with all your heart, with all your soul, with all your strength, and with all your mind," and "your neighbor as yourself." (*Mark 12:30*)

Solution on page 78

Scramble Challenge

1. Unscramble each word. 2. Add the letters from each gray box to the line at the bottom. 3. Decode the message.

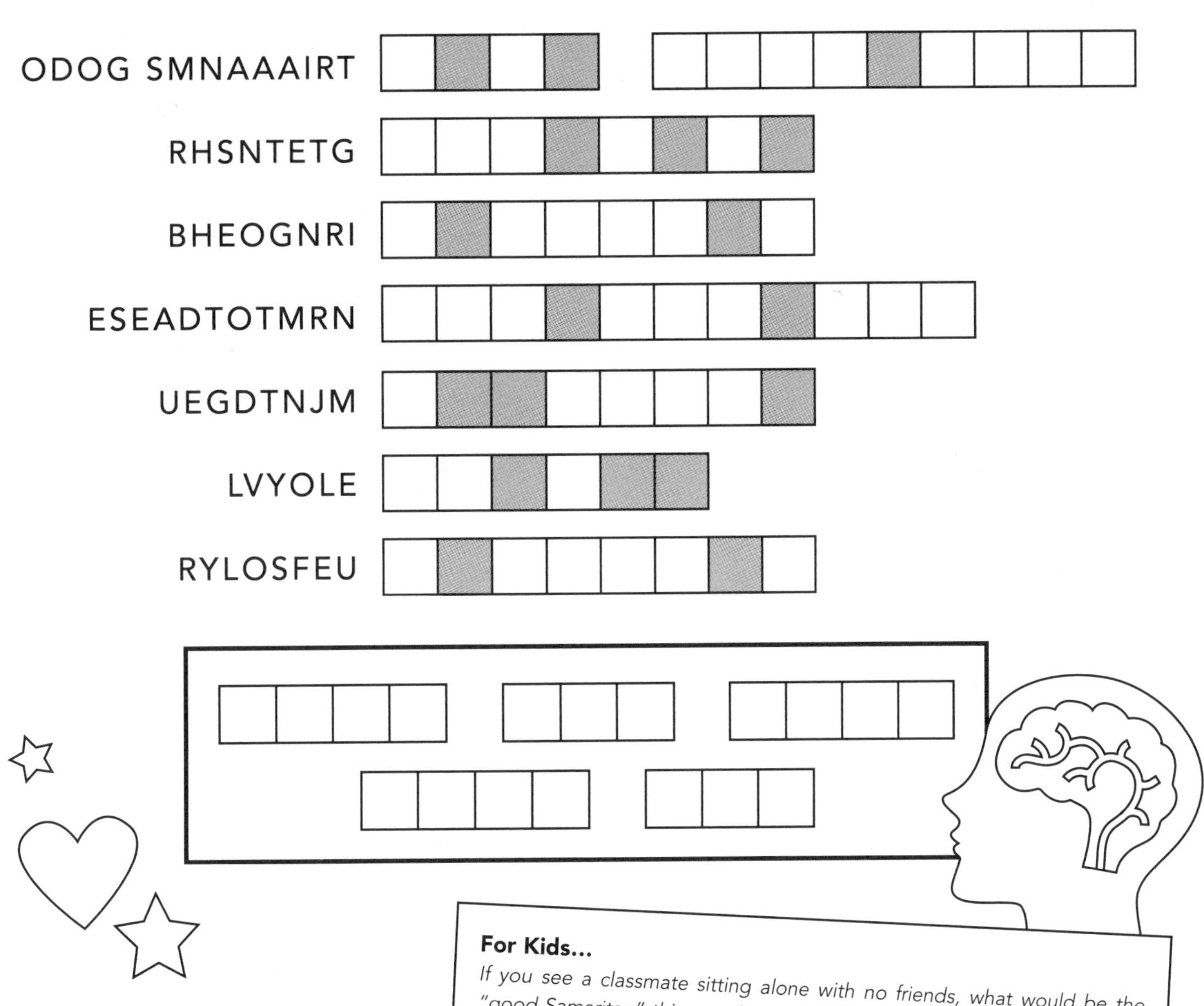

For Kids...

If you see a classmate sitting alone with no friends, what would be the "good Samaritan" thing to do? What would you want someone to do for you if you were sitting alone without any friends?

Jesus was approached by an expert of the law, asking him what he needed to do in order to have eternal life in heaven. Jesus paints a picture of a scenario, explaining how a man in need on the side of the road was avoided twice, but the third person took him in, treated his wounds, and cared for him like his own. Jesus asks which one of these people demonstrated loving their neighbor as themselves? Sometimes, we forget that everyone is worthy of love and God calls us to love freely, without judgment. This is called being a good Samaritan.

For Grown Ups...

When's the last time you stopped for the person sitting on the side of the road and demonstrated love to them either by giving them food, clothing, or guiding them to shelter in the area? In fact, take a day with your son or daughter and create a care bag that you can store in the back of your car with a toothbrush, granola bars, juice, socks, or anything else that you think a homeless person would need? Let's be prepared to love those that God places in our path, regardless of status or their situation.

Solution on page 78

Trace the Bread and the Cup

As they were eating, he took bread, blessed and broke it, gave it to them, and said, "Take it; this is my body." Then he took a cup, and after giving thanks, he gave it to them, and they all drank from it. He said to them, "This is my blood of the covenant, which is poured out for many." *(Mark 18:22–24)*

Trace and Color

The "Last Supper" is a key story in the Bible. All the disciples gathered around a table, not knowing it would be their last time with Jesus. Jesus took the cup and bread, and blessed it, providing a touching analogy of how to remember Him after He was gone. The bread represented the body of Jesus which would be broken for them. The cup would represent the blood that would be spilled for them. This is now what is called communion, a sacred ritual we still celebrate today. It is an important action we take—eating a piece of bread and drinking from the cup—a symbol of what Jesus did for us, sacrificing Himself for our sins.

For Kids...

Have you gone to church and ever wondered about the meaning behind communion? Next time this is offered to you, how can you show your respect to God through this action?

For Grown Ups...

Communion is a sacred reminder of what Jesus did for us. It's a great way to commune with God and thank Him for His love and sacrifice. Next time you are offered communion, take a moment and thank God for His love, mercy, and grace.

Follow the Numbers to Color the Cactus

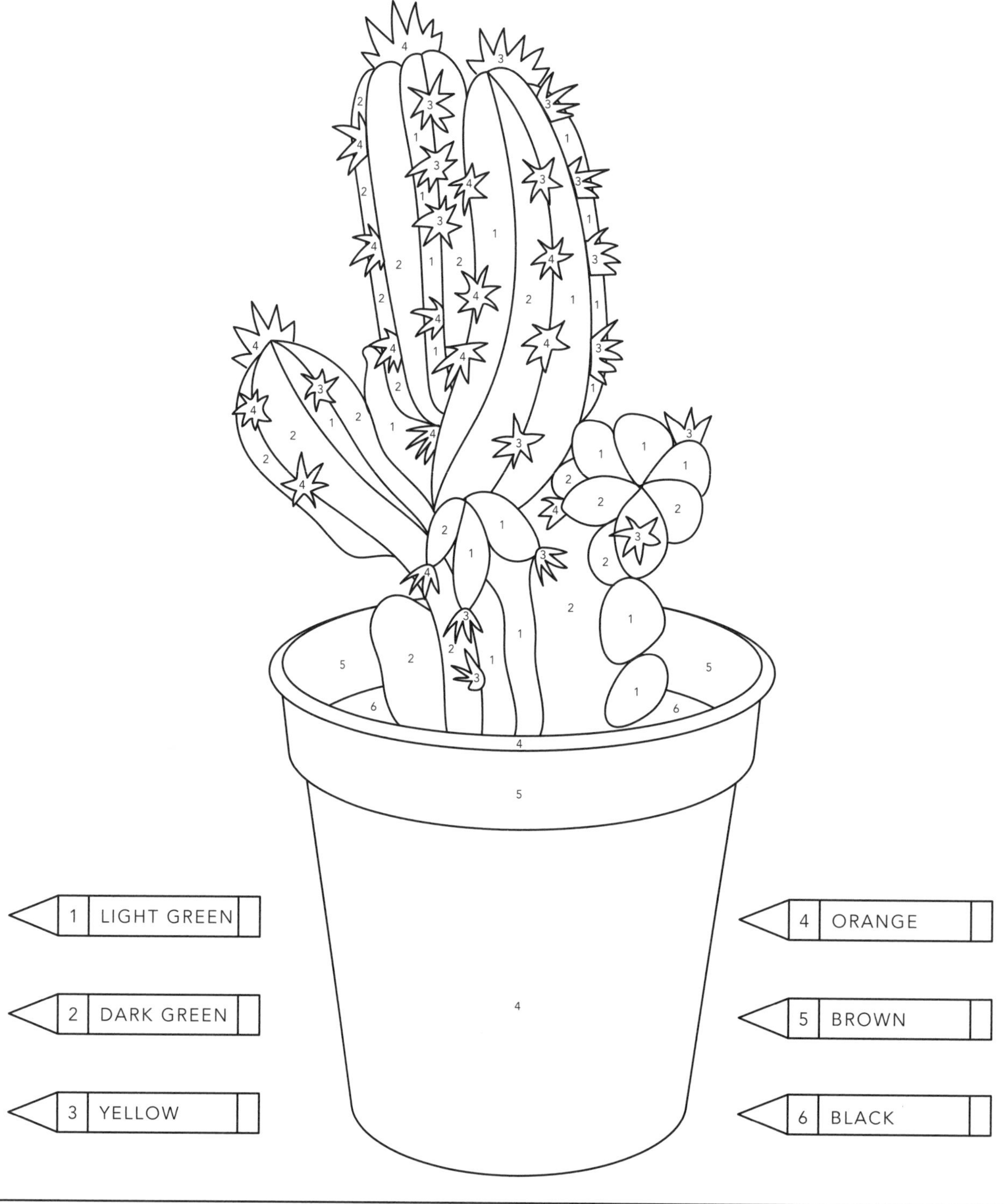

Then Jesus told him, "Go away, Satan! For it is written: Worship the Lord your God, and serve only him." *(Matthew 4:10)*

Color by Number

Did you know that even Jesus was tempted? Jesus went out into the desert—a dry, lonely place without any water or food for forty days (I would not recommend trying this). He was following the Spirit of God and was preparing His heart for the trials to come. The enemy of God—Satan—came to Him, trying to get Him to act selfishly by telling Jesus to turn rocks into bread, or have angels rescue Him from a fall, or bow down to Satan, himself. Jesus commanded Satan to leave, claiming the truth, "For it is written: Worship the Lord your God, and serve only him." Satan left and Jesus felt God's love surround Him. In the same way, we are always given a way out of temptation when we claim the truth of God's love for us over our hearts and minds.

For Kids...

Have you been tempted recently to do something bad (ie., lying, cheating, or saying mean things to someone else)? Sometimes saying out-loud, "Go away Satan!" can be helpful to turn our hearts back to God and keep ourselves free from sin. Try it next time!

For Grown Ups...

What temptation have you fallen into recently, and what can you do to overcome it next time temptation comes knocking?

What is under the water?

Use your imagination to draw what you think might live under the sea.

And climbing out of the boat, Peter started walking on the water and came toward Jesus. But when he saw the strength of the wind, he was afraid, and beginning to sink he cried out, "Lord, save me!" Immediately Jesus reached out his hand, caught hold of him, and said to him, "You of little faith, why did you doubt?" *(Matthew 14:29–31)*

Trace and Color

Can you imagine walking on water? On this particular day, Peter (one of the disciples of Jesus), found himself with the other disciples on a boat in the middle of the sea amidst a terrible storm. Waves pounded them this way and that as they tossed and turned on the boat. But suddenly, they saw a figure out on the water—Jesus! In faith, Peter asked to come onto the water with Him. Jesus told him to "Come," and Peter did the most amazing thing ever. He walked on water! But when Peter's focus drifted from Jesus to the massive winds around him, he allowed fear to creep in and started to sink in the waves. In the same way, we must not forget to take our eyes off Jesus when storms come in our lives. If we ever do, though, we can be assured that He will catch us when we start to sink.

For Kids...
When you're afraid, where is your focus? Where should you direct that focus to overcome the hard moments in life?

For Grown Ups...
Is there an area in your life where you may have taken your focus off Jesus? Is fear, anxiety, or confusion sweeping in? Turn your eyes back to Him and feel His hand pull you out of the stormy wind of life, once again.

Search and Find the Following Items in the Picture

When Daniel learned that the document had been signed, he went into his house. The windows in its upstairs room opened toward Jerusalem, and three times a day he got down on his knees, prayed, and gave thanks to his God, just as he had done before. *(Daniel 6:10)*

Solution on page 78

Search and Find

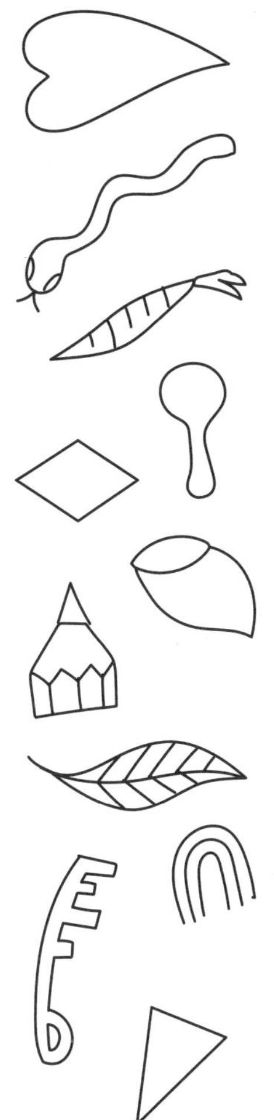

Daniel was a high ranking official next to the King, and he was devoted to God. Unfortunately, there were advisors to the King who seemed jealous of Daniel's position. Therefore, knowing Daniel's extreme devotion to God, they tricked the King to sign a law that no other worship should go to any other god or man for the next thirty days except for the King, otherwise they would be thrown in the lions' den. Well, this didn't stop Daniel from continuing in his worship to God. Sure enough, he was thrown to the lions. However, the most amazing thing happened the next morning. They found him alive! God protected Daniel from harm! We must not fear standing up for our belief and devotion to God, regardless of the consequences we might face in life.

For Kids...
What kind of scenarios do you have a tough time standing up for your faith in God?

For Grown Ups...
What kind of situation makes it difficult to stand up for your belief in God?

Solution on page 78

Color the Verse

The LORD spoke to Moses, "I have heard the complaints of the Israelites. Tell them: At twilight you will eat meat, and in the morning you will eat bread until you are full. Then you will know that I am the LORD your God." *(Exodus 16:11)*

Trace and Color the Verse

Moses was a man who led the Israelites out of slavery from Egypt. However, once the people were away from the city, they found themselves in the wilderness without food. Although God had recently demonstrated multiple miracles to these people, they began grumbling again, doubting God would provide for them, but God still met their needs. Meat (quail) and manna (bread) came to them each day. They weren't allowed to store it, which required them to trust that each day God would provide enough for them. This went on every day for forty years. Trust that God will provide for your daily needs. It won't be in excess**...**just enough to sustain and be satisfied.

For Kids...

Have you found yourself grumbling because you don't have enough toys, clothes, or something else you really want? Did you know that everything you have is a blessing? What blessings can you thank God for right now?

For Grown Ups...

Have you found yourself grumbling because you don't have a nice enough house, nice enough car, or frustrated that you don't have more when God has given you more than enough to sustain you? What can you thank God for right now?

Judges 4 Crossword

Read the verses at the bottom of the page for clues.

Across

3. Group of soldiers
5. Prophetess
6. Horse carriage used in battle

Down

1. Chosen people
2. Weapon
4. Respected military leader

Then Deborah said to Barak, "Go! This is the day the Lord has handed Sisera over to you. Hasn't the Lord gone before you?" So Barak came down from Mount Tabor with ten thousand men following him...Barak pursued the chariots and the army as far as Harosheth of the Nations, and the whole army of Sisera fell by the sword; not a single man was left. *(Judges 4 :14; 16)*

Solution on page 79

Judges 4 Crossword

Hint: read all of Judges 4.

Across

1. Disagreements
3. Hill country
5. Who Barak summoned
6. Sending out troops
7. Harmony
8. God
10. Scared
11. Metal
12. Used to fasten a tent
15. Leader of army
16. Warm covering
18. One
19. Mountain in Israel
21. Portable canvas shelter
22. A Kenite

Down

2. Called
4. Type of tree
5. Location of oak tree
8. Husband of Deborah
9. Foot soliders
13. Dominance
14. Wife of Heber
16. Son of Abinoam
17. Opposite of decrease
18. Commander of army
20. Quenches thirst
22. Respect

Deborah was a woman of high authority, a prophetess of her time. She summoned Barak, a respected military leader, and shared with him the message she received from God. She told him to take ten thousand men and attack a neighboring country that was treating God's chosen people, the Israelites, poorly. Barak believed Deborah's leadership and spiritual insights about what God had told her. Sure enough, they worked together, trusting one another, to bring about a successful outcome. Working together we can overcome obstacles, help point each other on the right path and fulfill the things God wants us to do here on earth.

For Kids...

How can you work together with your classmates, parents, or other people in your life to complete the tasks before you?

For Grown Ups...

I've seen first hand how much more impactful and successful we are when we seek to work together to steward positive ideas or move one another forward and become successful at building up God's kingdom here on earth. What's an area of your life you've been trying to do things on your own that maybe would work better if you worked with another person or organization to create a better outcome?

Solution on page 79

Decode the Word

Match the shapes to the letter in the key.

____ ____ ____ ____ ____ ____ ____ ____ ____

○ ⬡ □ ▲ ● ■ △ ⬡ ⬢

○ C	▲ N	● S
■ E	⬡ O	□ U
△ L	⬢ R	

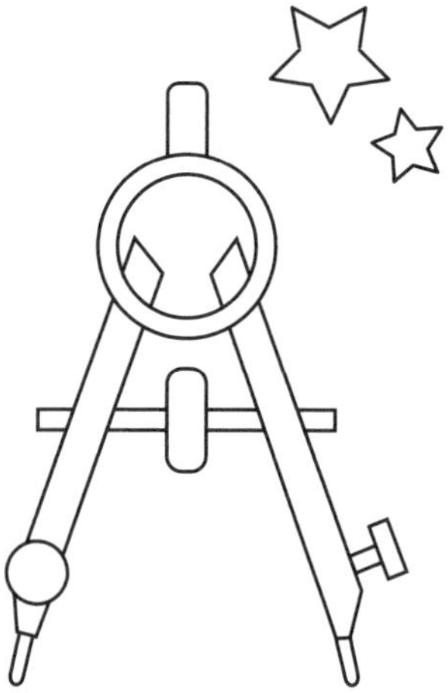

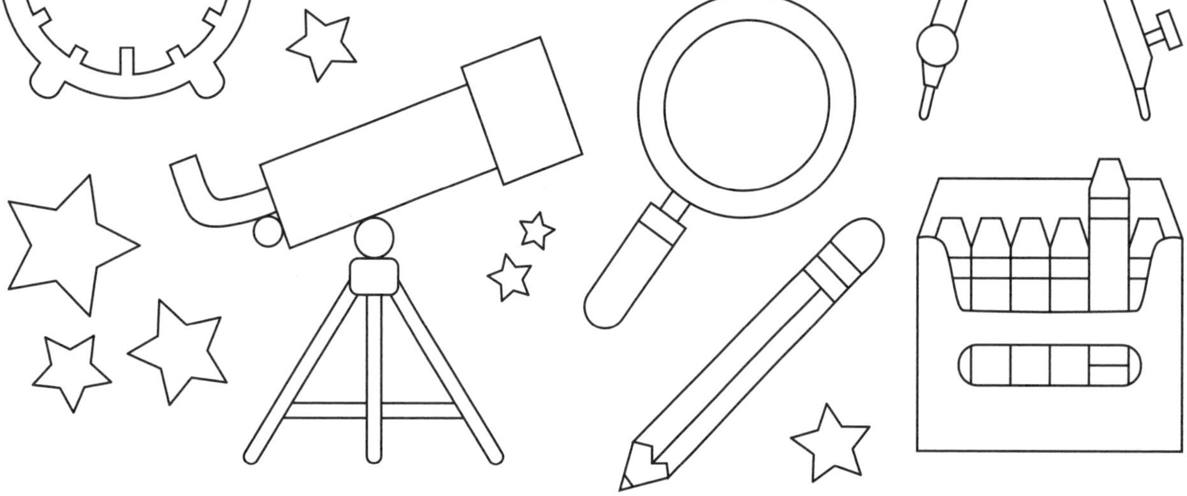

"Nevertheless, I am telling you the truth. It is for your benefit that I go away, because if I don't go away the Counselor will not come to you. If I go, I will send him to you." *(John 16:7)*

Solution on page 80

Fill in the letters that correspond to the numbers below the blanks to solve the phrase.

A	B	C	D	E	F	G	H	I	J	K	L	M	N	O	P	Q	R	S	T	U	V	W	X	Y	Z
	23					14			5					22			21	2							

_ _ _ _ R _ _ _ _ _ S S ,   _   _ _   _ _ _ _ _ _ G   _ O _
13 17 25 17 21 9 7 17 18 17 2 2 ,   11   10 24   9 17 18 18 11 13 14   20 22 1

_ _ _   _ R _ _ _   _ _   _ S   _ O R   _ O _ R
9 7 17   9 21 1 9 7   11 9   11 2   26 22 21   20 22 1 21

B _ _ _ _ _ _   _ _ _ _   _   G O   _ _ _ _ ,
23 17 13 17 26 11 9   9 7 10 9   11   14 22   10 3 10 20 ,

B _ _ _ _ S _   _ _   _   _ O _ _   G O   _ _ _ _   _ _ _
23 17 16 10 1 2 17   11 26   11   8 22 13 9   14 22   10 3 10 20   9 7 17

_ O _ _ S _ _ O R   _ _ _ _   _ O _   _ O _ _   _ O
16 22 1 13 2 17 18 22 21   3 11 18 18   13 22 9   16 22 24 17   9 22

_ O _ .   _ _   _   G O ,   _   _ _ _ _   S _ _ _   _ _ _
20 22 1 .   11 26   11   14 22 ,   11   3 11 18 18   2 17 13 8   7 11 24

T _   _ O _ .   J O _ _   16:7
9 22   20 22 1 .   5 22 7 13

Before Jesus was crucified on the cross, He spoke about how the Counselor will come and that it is even good for us that Jesus leaves and the Counselor comes. The Counselor is the Holy Spirit. Why is the Holy Spirit coming a benefit? It is because we have the Holy Spirit wherever we go within us when we believe and accept a personal relationship with Him! Do you recognize that you have access to the mighty power of the Holy Spirit in your life, right now, wherever you are? He is with you and will never leave you. He will empower you to love others and live a life worth living when you trust and follow His guidance.

For Kids...
Have you, or the one across from you, ever asked the Holy Spirit into your heart? All you have to do is pray and accept Jesus as your Savior!

For Grown Ups...
If you were face-to-face with the living, breathing Jesus right now, and He said that it's better if He leaves so the Holy Spirit can come, would you believe Him? We must remember the power we have obtained with the Holy Spirit is in us wherever we go.

Solution on page 80

2 Kings 5:2–3 Word Scramble

Unscramble each word. Use the verse at the bottom of the page for clues!

CGERA ____________________

AHLE ____________________

VERRI ____________________

DGO ____________________

ISNK ____________________

RGLI ____________________

RCEU ____________________

SWHA ____________________

Aram had gone on raids and brought back from the land of Israel a young girl who served Naaman's wife. She said to her mistress, "If only my master were with the prophet who is in Samaria, he would cure him of his skin disease." *(2 Kings 5:2–3)*

Solution on page 81

Scramble Challenge

1. Unscramble each word. **2.** Add the letters from each gray box to the line at the bottom. **3.** Decode the message.

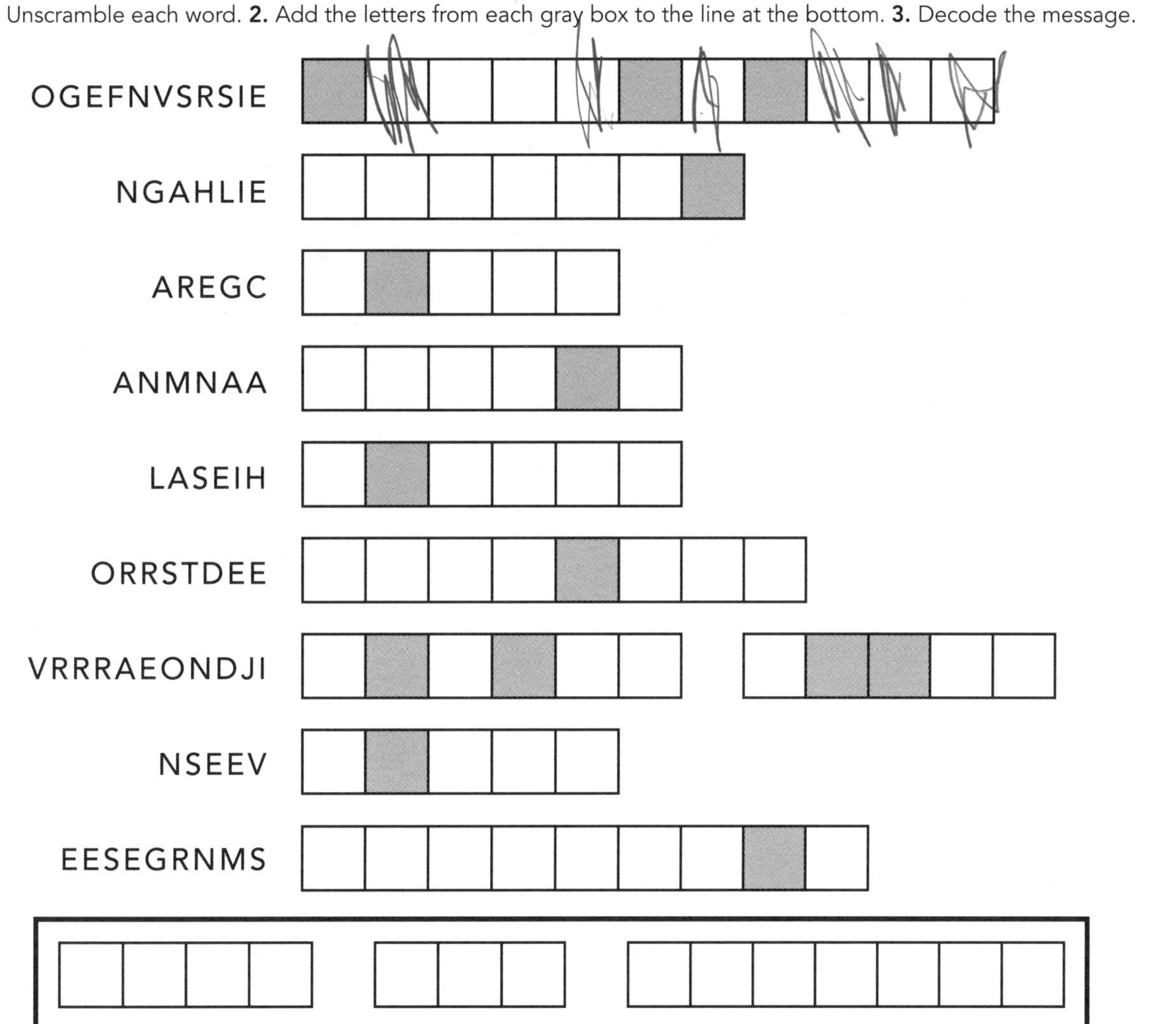

Forgiving and helping someone that has treated you poorly is easier said than done. In the book of 2 Kings, there was a little servant girl who was forced to serve a man named Naaman. He was considered to be a very important man to the king at that time. Sadly, this girl was taken away from her home as the king conquered areas of the land where she lived. Her life was spared only to become a slave to Naaman and his wife. One day, Naaman grew sick with leprosy—a skin disease that's painful, generates ugly sores and causes deformities. He needed help, but no one knew what to do—except the slave girl. She knew how Naaman could be healed. But why would she want to help him? She had every right to hate him. Instead, she chose to forgive him and helped him find healing. God healed Naaman through an obedient act of faith. He listened to this slave girl, followed her instructions to full healing, and even more importantly, he discovered the truth about God in the process.

For Kids...

Is there someone you need to forgive in your life that you feel has mistreated you? What if your forgiveness softens that person's heart and compels them to discover God's forgiveness?

For Grown Ups...

What if we started treating everyone with love and forgave their wrong actions towards us? Wouldn't these make them curious about your faith in God that enables you to love and forgive? How can you live this out daily?

Solution on page 81

Color the Verse

"But even if he does not rescue us, we want you as king to know that we will not serve your gods or worship the gold statue you set up." *(Daniel 3:18)*

Trace and Color the Verse

Three men—Shadrach, Meshach, and Abednego—were asked to bow down to a gold statue King Nebuchadnezzar created. If they didn't, they would be thrown in a blazing furnace. Everyone else did as they were told, except for Shadrach, Meshach, and Abednego. They continued to proclaim their belief in the one true God and claimed that they would be saved from the blazing furnace. Even if they wouldn't be saved, they made it clear that they still believed in Gods goodness and would not bow down to King Nebuchadnezzar, no matter what. They would worship only God Himself, even if things didn't go the way they hoped it would.

For Kids...

If someone asked you to choose between a spot in the popular crowd and reject your belief in God OR being unpopular and mistreated but still proclaiming your belief in God..., which would you choose?

For Grown Ups...

What "but if not" moment have you had in your own life when things didn't go as planned, and it tested your faith in God?

Leah Word Search

Search for the words in the key.

When the LORD saw that Leah was unloved, he opened her womb. (*Genesis 29:31*)

Solution on page 82

Luke 15 Word Search

- CHERISHED
- DESIRED
- FELT
- GENESIS
- LAVISHED
- LEAH
- LIFE
- OPENED
- REMINDERS
- SIGNIFICANT
- SPECIAL
- TALENTS
- THROUGH

L	D	W	A	S	N	G	T	O	W	E	S	A	C	V	M	S	S	E	Y	T	G	U	I	N
A	T	E	P	N	E	C	H	E	R	I	S	H	E	D	Q	P	J	S	G	P	O	E	W	T
W	C	O	M	G	P	H	R	A	M	G	I	Q	T	S	E	P	K	R	O	R	N	S	H	G
G	Y	P	T	E	L	Q	O	H	L	F	G	W	A	C	A	U	R	E	E	S	T	I	I	O
L	I	H	G	P	F	U	U	P	D	U	H	M	I	W	H	G	T	M	I	X	A	G	H	Q
D	E	J	O	I	C	E	G	U	A	P	T	A	H	A	S	D	E	I	O	L	I	N	U	D
E	W	P	R	A	B	J	H	L	I	Y	L	S	K	U	I	N	A	N	P	T	G	I	P	S
S	G	T	Q	Y	G	O	G	E	A	P	O	B	V	L	T	U	F	D	N	F	K	F	O	U
I	L	I	U	F	T	L	H	A	G	V	U	Y	C	A	B	Q	H	E	A	W	H	I	T	N
R	R	E	P	G	O	M	U	H	E	M	I	X	N	P	R	O	M	R	J	X	C	C	E	G
E	L	X	I	T	W	J	G	I	U	L	N	S	D	S	Z	W	K	S	K	R	I	A	H	L
D	Y	R	E	O	U	A	E	V	A	T	E	B	H	A	D	P	S	D	T	F	G	N	I	E
O	P	E	N	E	D	Y	K	L	O	E	S	P	G	E	N	E	S	I	S	W	E	T	L	J
I	O	P	L	E	Z	C	P	D	G	I	S	J	A	S	D	Y	D	K	G	A	O	X	T	K
B	M	K	S	T	M	G	O	A	Q	W	Y	L	Z	M	J	E	C	D	Y	T	W	J	U	H
N	I	R	M	T	A	L	E	N	T	S	O	K	Q	A	E	S	T	O	X	N	L	A	P	O
O	C	Q	Y	E	W	G	N	S	T	A	P	I	P	E	F	D	A	P	I	B	H	K	I	M
X	E	U	V	R	S	D	P	C	W	E	B	N	G	W	I	H	R	E	F	O	A	G	X	E
S	T	I	B	W	L	J	O	F	D	U	R	L	F	E	L	T	S	D	C	L	I	R	T	W
P	Q	L	K	A	T	G	Y	I	R	Z	O	K	A	Q	Y	T	E	P	H	E	R	D	F	G

Have you ever felt unloved or unseen? Perhaps you've been looked over by friends or family? Maybe you've gone through a difficult season? Leah felt this exact same way. She had a sister who seemed to have it all: looks, love, and lavished with gifts. Leah, however, always came second. God, seeing her difficulties, brought a gift to her life; she was able to have children. She was able to experience God's love in a way that helped her feel seen, cherished, and desired, regardless of the lack of love and affection around her. Although not everything will go the way we hope in life, God is always giving us gifts if we have the eyes to see His love for us.

For Kids...

Look around you, what gifts do you see that God has given you to demonstrate His love for you? (i.e. sunrise, the ability to sing, running fast, making people laugh, or creatively acting out the stories in your mind?)

For Grown Ups...

You may feel overlooked in one area of life—not the best singer, cook, or creative thinker—but we all have gifts that God has given us that we might have overlooked ourselves! Think about what natural skills or talents you have. What special talents, provisions, or tangible reminders has God given you as expressions of His great love for you?

Solution on page 82

Connect the Dots to Complete the Temple

Before the lamp of God had gone out, Samuel was lying down in the temple of the LORD, where the ark of God was located. Then the LORD called Samuel, and he answered, "Here I am." *(1 Samuel 3:3–4)*

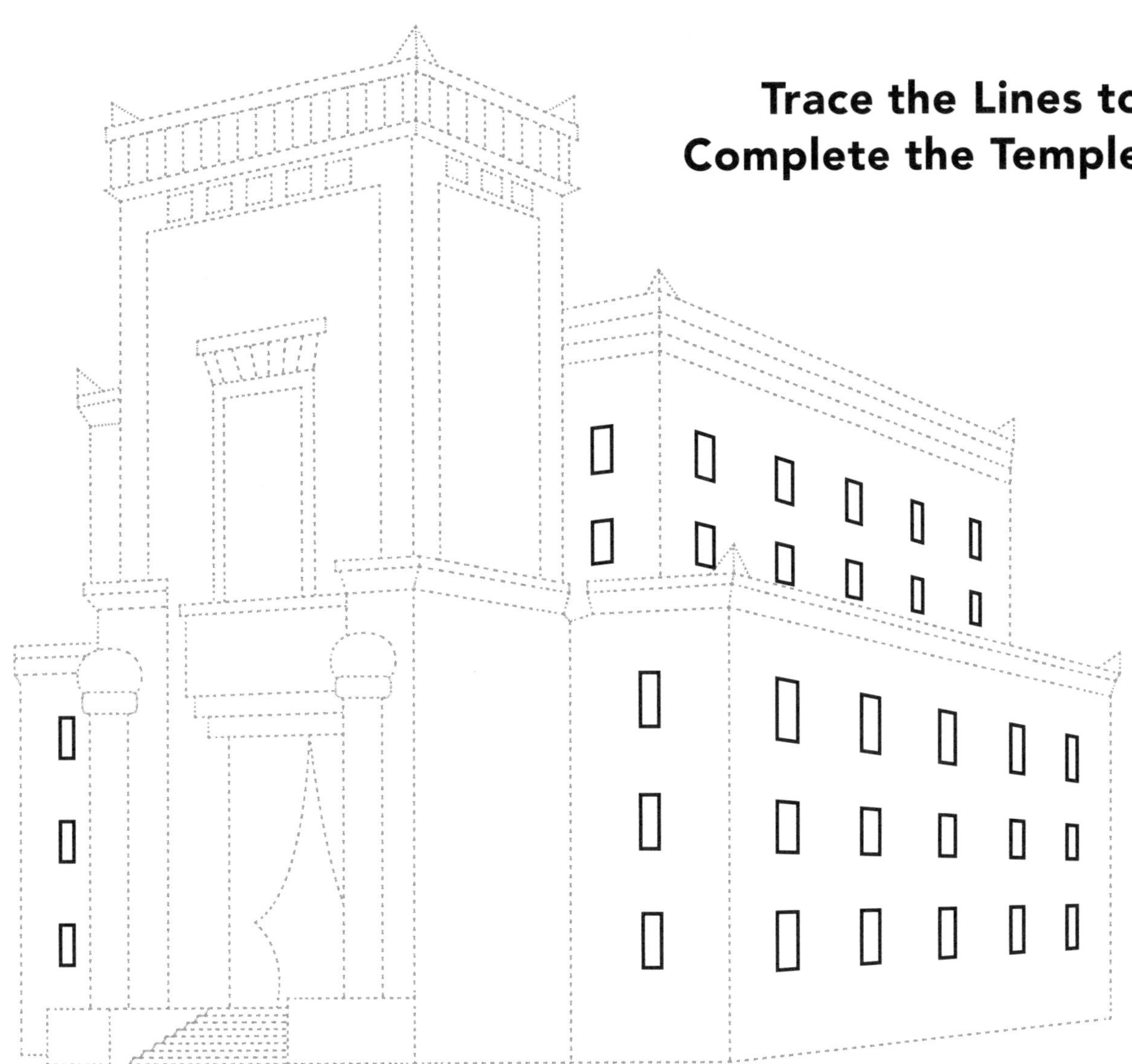

Trace the Lines to Complete the Temple

According to biblical history, there was a boy named Samuel who was eleven years old and didn't yet know God. God, however, spoke to him four times in the stillness of the temple. The first two times Samuel thought it was Eli—a man he served at the temple. The third time, Eli realized it was God speaking to Samuel. Eli told Samuel to respond back to God. So, on the fourth time, God spoke and Samuel responded, receiving what God wanted him to know. No matter how old, or young, you are, God can and will speak to you. We must be sensitive to His voice. The more you seek to know Him the more you will know His voice when He is speaking to you in personal ways.

For Kids...

Have you ever sensed God speaking to your heart? No matter your age, the Holy Spirit of God can speak to our hearts, especially if we are quiet enough to listen (Psalm 46:10; Matthew 10:19–20).

For Grown Ups...

God can speak to us in multiple ways—through visions, dreams, other people, and most often in our hearts or minds if we let Him (John 14:26; 1 Thess. 5:19; Gal. 5:16). When you're driving in the car this week, turn off the radio, or get in a quiet place in your house, and ask God if He has something to say to you! The more you do this, the more you will tune in to hear His voice in your life.

Finish the Drawing

Add more houses to the city.

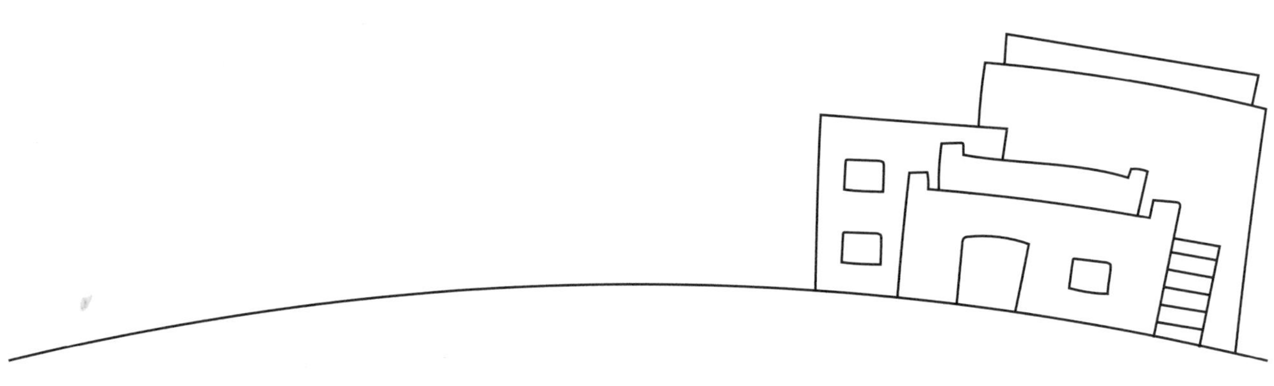

Each of the priests made repairs above the Horse Gate, each opposite his own house. (*Nehemiah 3:28*)

Draw the Mirror Image of the City

What if we all worked together to help each other instead of looking out for ourselves? This is what the priests did in the book of Nehemiah, serving one another to help rebuild walls, buildings, and other structures that were previously destroyed. The sons of Hassenaah built the Fish Gate while others made repairs. The various tribes repaired one another's houses without quarrel, envy or a "what's in it for me" attitude. In the same way, let's look out for each other- offering our help to a neighbor whose fence is broken or dropping off groceries for someone who is ill and can't travel or serving in some way to help lift the burden of others. When you do this for others, it's likely it will come back around to you when you need help too.

For Kids...
Think of someone in your neighborhood or class that has a need you can help fulfill for them. Can you help mow their grass, wheel out their trash, or donate a few toys you're not playing with anymore?

For Grown Ups...
Work together with your child to figure out a way you both can serve the needs of family or friends nearby. Is there someone ill that needs groceries, something needing repaired in their house you can easily fix, or are there toys you aren't using you can donate?

Color the Verse

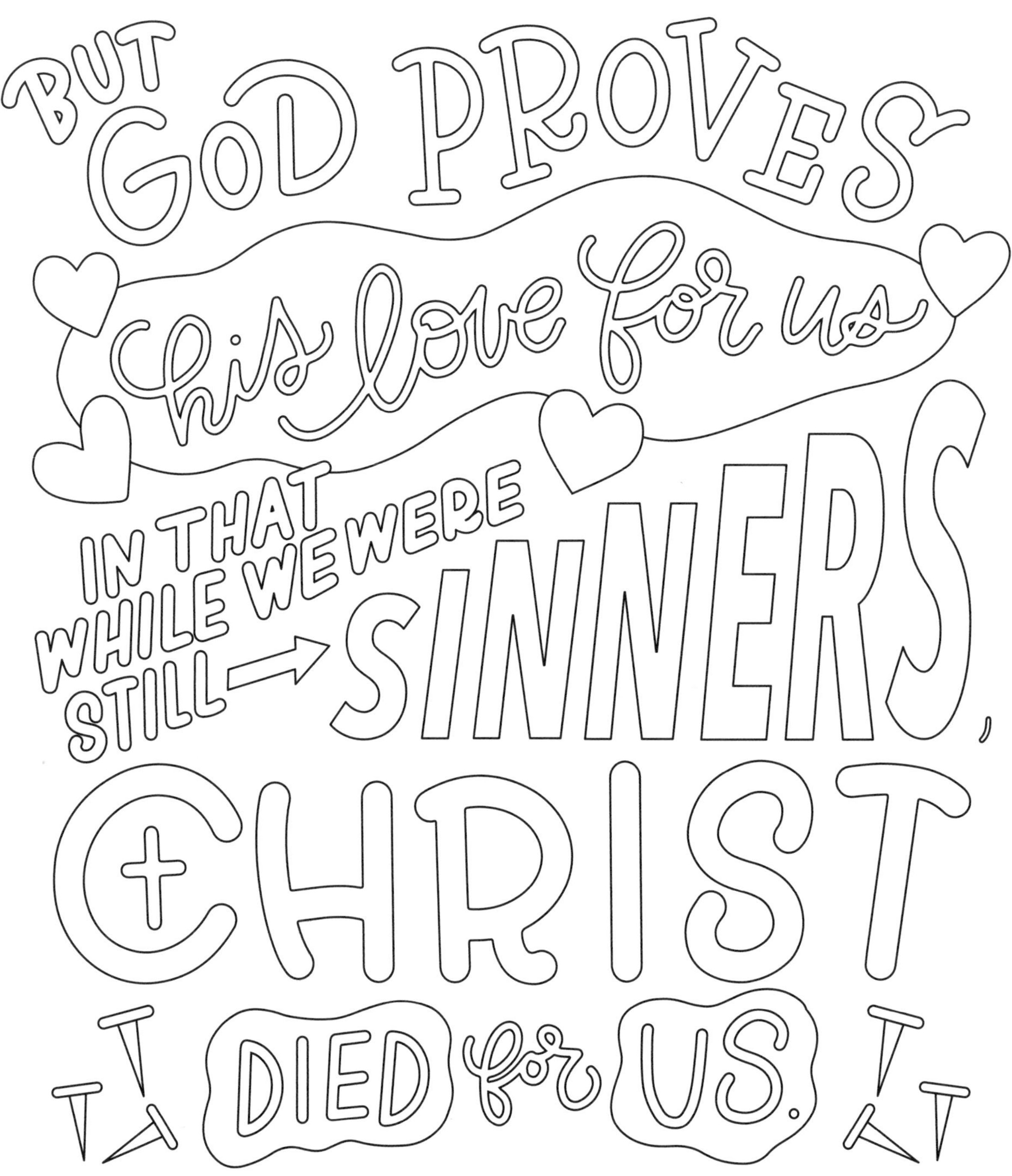

For rarely will someone die for a just person—though for a good person perhaps someone might even dare to die. But God proves his own love for us in that while we were still sinners, Christ died for us. (*Romans 5:7–8*)

Trace and Color the Verse

Important leaders, like the president, are often assigned bodyguards to protect them from harm, even to the point of death. While the bodyguard's job may be to take a bullet for someone, rarely will someone die for another person willingly. However, we see this demonstration through Jesus, who willingly sacrificed Himself on the cross, not just for one person, but for every person on Earth. Without His sacrifice, and the acceptance of His sacrifice, we would forever be separated from God. God made a way through His Son, Jesus, to take the "bullet" for us, enabling us to live with God in heaven for eternity. This is true love, my friend.

For Kids...
How does the unconditional love of Jesus through His sacrifice make you feel? Happy, sad, glad, thankful?

For Grown Ups...
How does this understanding that Jesus took a "bullet" for you—giving you the gift of eternal life—make you feel? Pray and reflect on this right now.

Psalm 139 Word Search

Search for the words in the key.

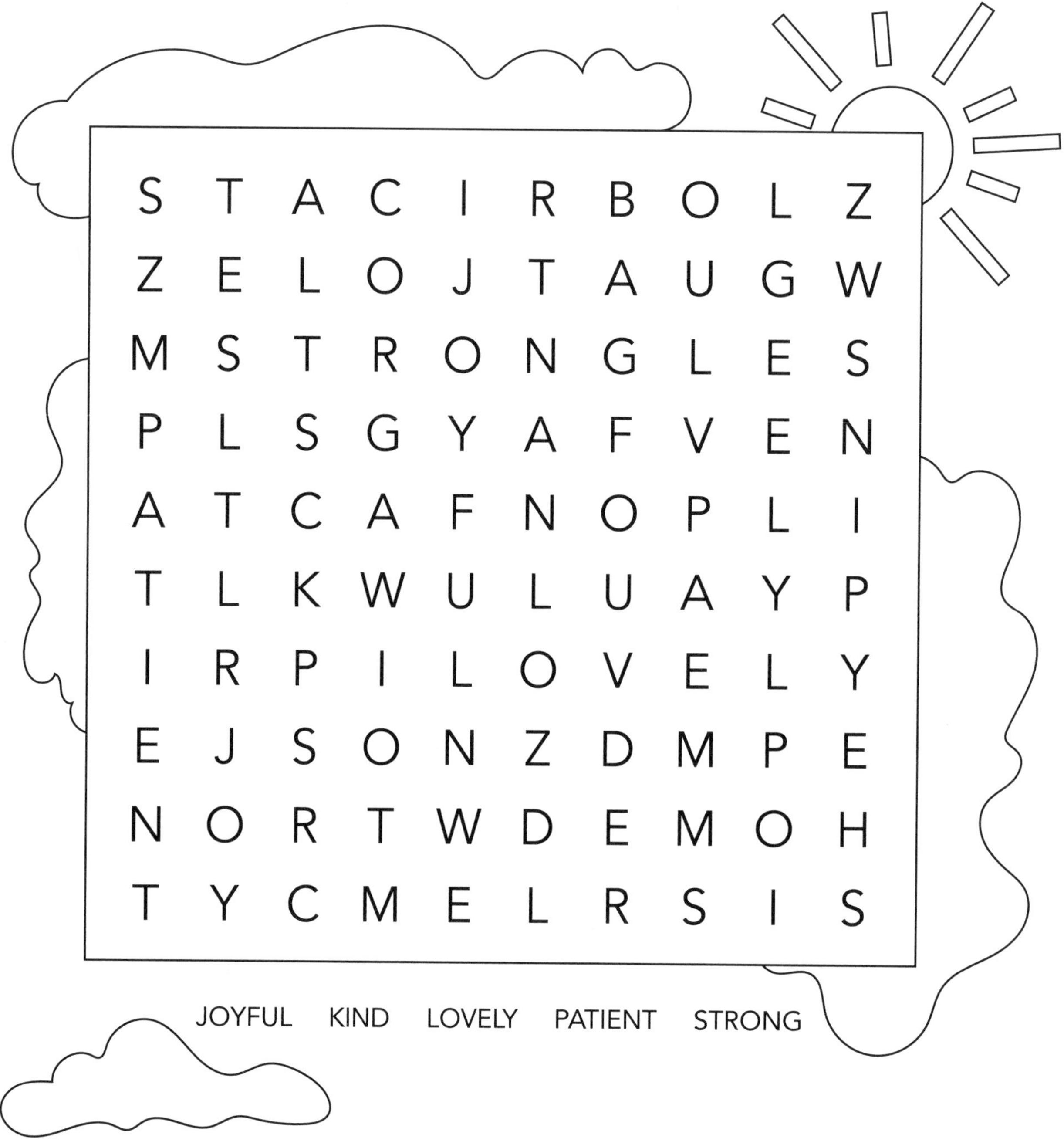

I will praise you because I have been remarkably and wondrously made. Your works are wondrous, and I know this very well. *(Psalm 139:14)*

Solution on page 83

Psalm 139 Word Search

L D W A S B G K O W E S A C V M A R V E L O U S S
A T E C H E R I S H E D U I P Q U J S G P O E W T
W C O M G L H R A M G I Q T F V P K X O R N F H G
G Y P T E O Q F H L F R E M A R K A B L E T L I O
L I H G P V U M P D U H M O I H G T E I X A G H Q
B E J T H E E C U A P T I H T S T R O N G L J U D
A W P R A D J X T C Y E S K H I N A S P T G Q P S
Y G T Q Y H O G Y R P O B V F T U F T N F K S O U
M L I U F T W I S E R M Y C U B Q H Y A W H F T N
Y R E P G O M U A A M S X S L R O M R J X C S E G
Q L X I K W J D I T L N C O S Z W K V K R I O H A
U Y R E O U E E V E T T V Y A D P S D T F G B I M
Q D C J N S Y K L D E E P I L Q A T B N K I N D A
I O P L O Z C O D G L S J A S U T D K G L R K E Z
B M K P N Y G O A Y W Y L Z M J I C D Y T W J U I
N I R M H Y F Z E R J O K Q A P E T O X N L A P N
O U Q Y E W G U S T D P I P E T N A P I B H K I G
P E U V R S D P L W E B N G W O T R E F O A G X E
S T I B W L J O F D U R L F B U H S D C L I R T W
P Q L K A T G Y I R Z O K E D S P E L H Q R D F G

AMAZING	FAITHFUL	MARVELOUS	REMARKABLE
BELOVED	JOYFUL	PATIENT	STRONG
CHERISHED	KIND	PURPOSED	WISE
CREATED	LOVELY		

God created the world, and everything in it. He created us in His image (Genesis 1:27) and said it was all good! But often, we forget how remarkably and wonderfully made we truly are. We let the world tell us we aren't good enough, talented enough, or attractive enough. Instead, we must believe in the truth that God created each and every one of us intentionally, with a unique purpose. We are able to praise God when we remember that we are remarkably and wondrously made in His image.

For Kids...
Do you know that God remarkably and wondrously made you? God didn't mess up making you. Tell yourself over and over again: "I am an amazing child of God!"

For Grown Ups...
We often forget how God sees us: remarkably and wondrously made. Speak life-giving, positive words over yourself the way God would! Do this now. (ie., "I am beloved; I am cherished; I have a purpose; I am strong!)

Solution on page 83

Follow the Numbers to Color the Fire

God has raised this Jesus; we are all witnesses of this. Therefore, since he has been exalted to the right hand of God and has received from the Father the promised Holy Spirit, he has poured out what you both see and hear. *(Acts 2:32–33)*

Color by Number

1 light yellow
2 dark yellow
3 light orange
4 dark orange
5 light red
6 dark red

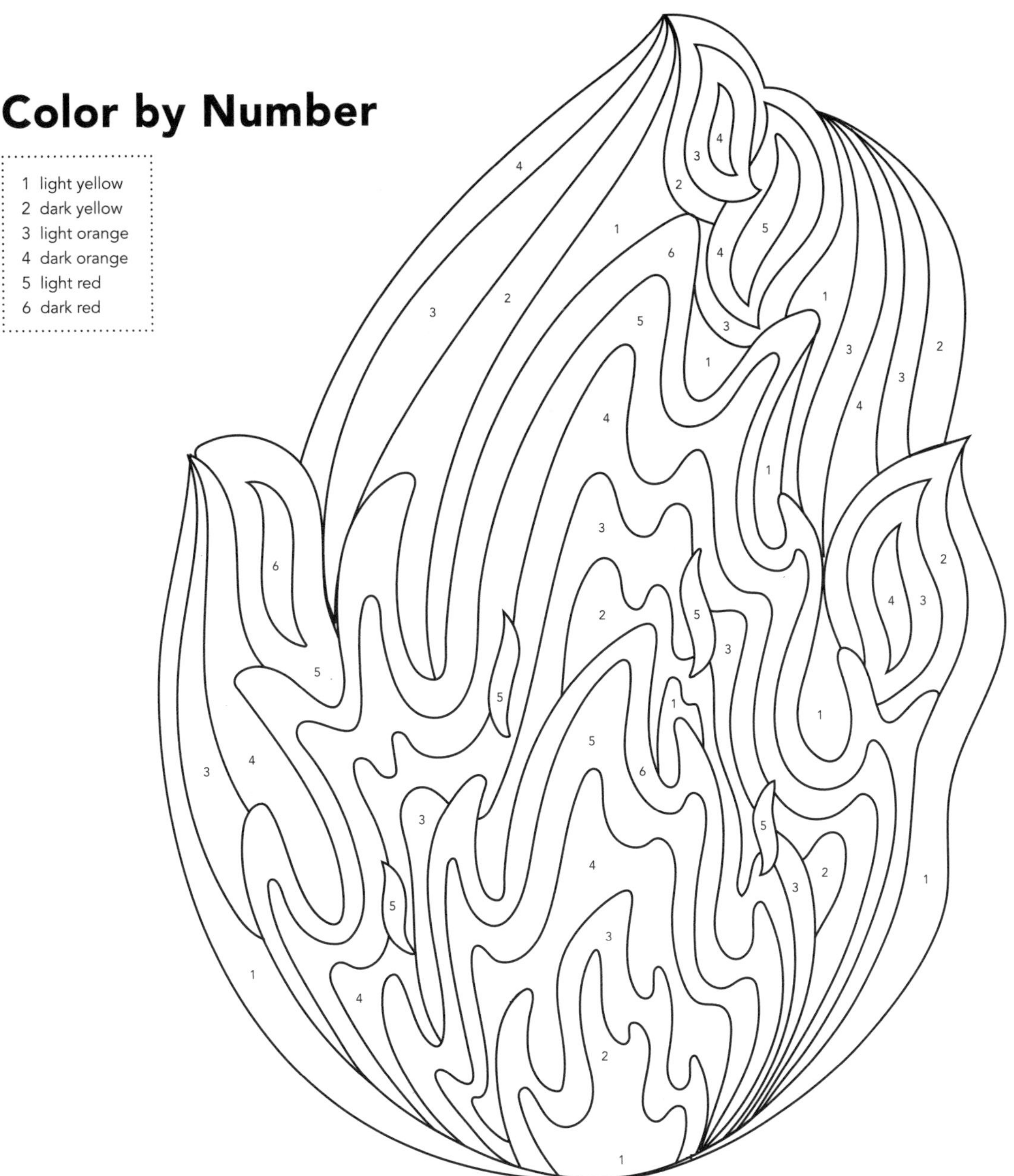

In Acts 2, we read about the day of Pentecost. A rushing wind came over a group of one hundred and twenty people, including the disciples, as flames rested on each one of their heads. They were all filled with the Holy Spirit in this moment. This enabled and compelled them to perform miracles, sell their possessions, break bread together, and be in community with one another. They were joyful despite their circumstances because they were filled with the love and awe of God. What a gift we've been given. The Holy Spirit enables us to love and serve others in radical ways.

For Kids...
How can you love and serve someone else today in a radical way? When you let the Holy Spirit lead, radical love is possible.

For Grown Ups...
How are you letting the Holy Spirit lead in your life? What does it look like to let the Holy Spirit work in your life?

Find Nine Differences Between the Pictures

"So if I, your Lord and Teacher, have washed your feet, you also ought to wash one another's feet. For I have given you an example, that you also should do just as I have done for you." *(John 13:14–15)*

Solution on page 84

Find eighteen differences between the pictures.

It was common to have a basin of water by the door to wash your feet during that time. Unlike the nicely paved sidewalks in shoes that we wear today, most people travelled on dirt roads in sandals. Typically, a servant or host would wash the guest's feet. However, in this story, Jesus (the Almighty God in flesh), knelt and began washing Peter's filthy feet. Jesus did this to demonstrate that we should serve one another, regardless of our status, color, gender, or anything else that might separate us. Not one is better than the other. His hope was that we would connect-the-dots through this example and serve each other in love without judgment.

For Kids...
When your parents ask you to help around the house, pick up your toys, or make your bed, do you grumble and complain about it or do you serve willingly? Look for ways this week to help, even if it's not your job to do so.

For Grown Ups...
When you see a homeless person, do you look away or do you lean in and see how you can serve them? We are all children of God. Not one is better than another. Let's find ways to serve others around us.

Solution on page 85

Luke 8:49–50 Word Scramble

Unscramble each word. Use the verse at the bottom of the page for clues!

While he was still speaking, someone came from the synagogue leader's house and said, "Your daughter is dead. Don't bother the teacher anymore." When Jesus heard it, he answered him, "Don't be afraid. Only believe, and she will be saved." *(Luke 8:49–50)*

Solution on page 86

Scramble Challenge

1. Unscramble each word. **2.** Add the letters from each gray box to the line at the bottom. **3.** Decode the message.

In Luke 8 there was a crowd of people swarming around Jesus. People knew of His power and the miracles He was performing. A man named Jairus asked Him to come to his home and heal his sick and dying daughter. As Jesus began making His way through the crowds to this girl, He didn't seem to be in a hurry and ended up helping someone else, taking up precious time, which prevented Him from reaching the child before she passed away. However, Jesus wasn't really late. He was readying himself to perform yet another miracle even greater than all the others. He told Jairus, "only believe and she will be saved." The crowd laughed at Him because no one had ever brought a dead person back to life. However, Jesus entered the room, asked her to "get up," and she was revived! Sometimes we believe God is taking too long, but perhaps He wants to demonstrate His power to you in even more awe-inspiring ways.

For Kids...
Waiting is hard. However, why is waiting on God's timing so important? In fact, do you think waiting patiently might lead to something even better?

For Grown Ups...
*What areas of your life are you waiting for God to show up? What can you do as you trust Him in the waiting? (*hint: pray, listen, read the Bible)*

Solution on page 86

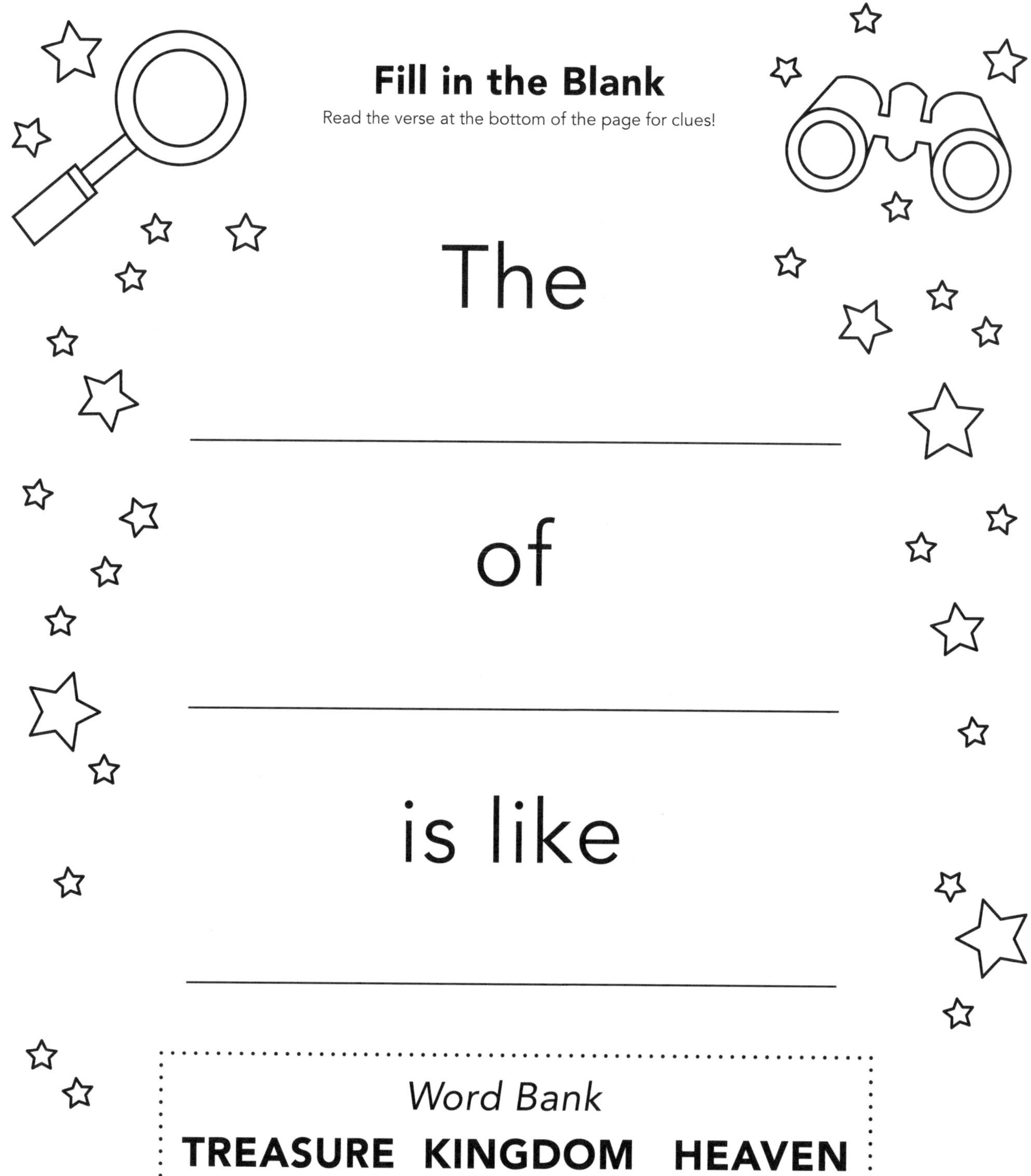

Fill in the Blank

Read the verse at the bottom of the page for clues!

The

____

of

____

is like

____

Word Bank

TREASURE KINGDOM HEAVEN

"The kingdom of heaven is like treasure, buried in a field, that a man found and reburied. Then in his joy he goes and sells everything he has and buys that field." (*Matthew 13:44*)

Solution on page 86

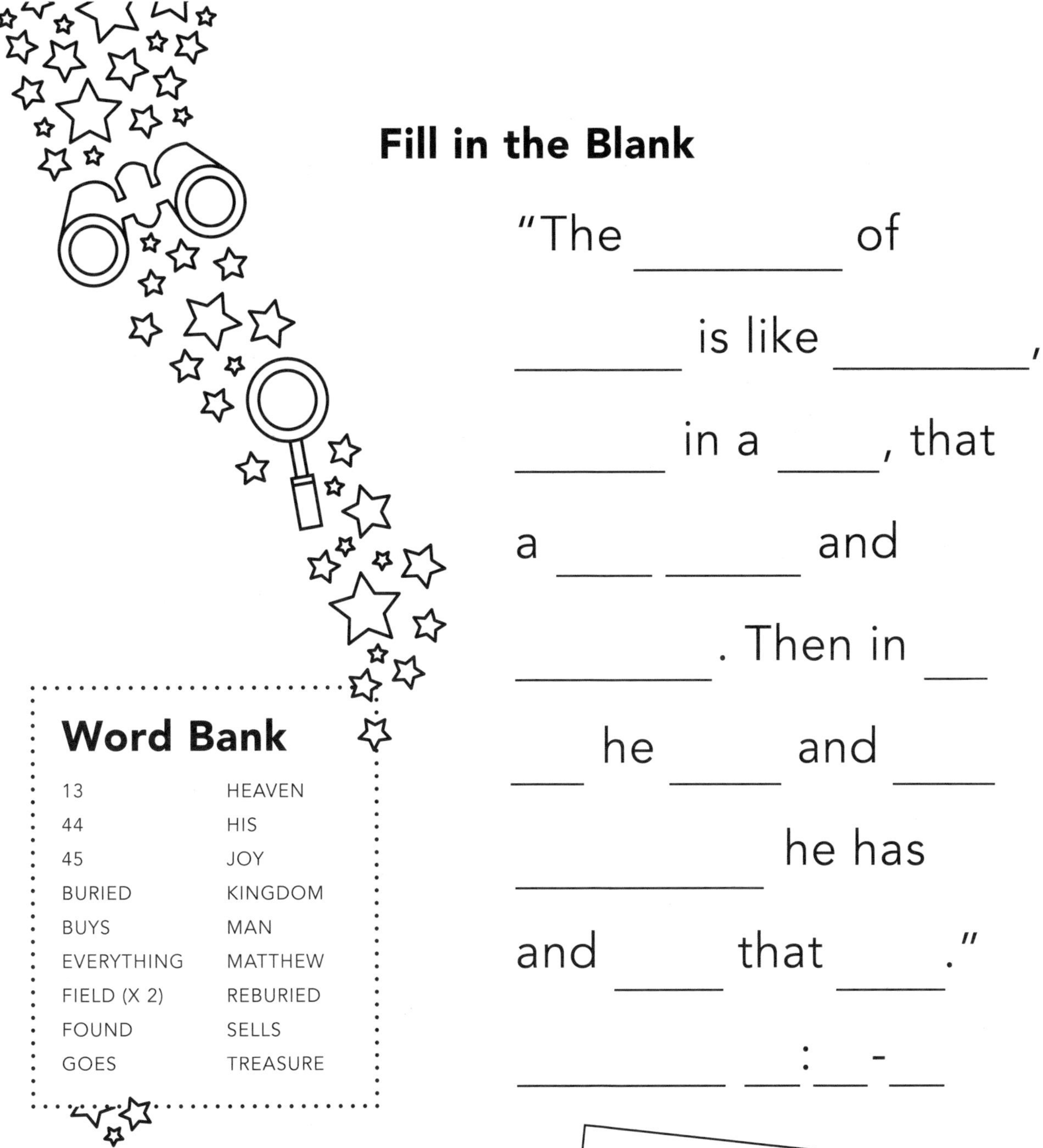

Fill in the Blank

"The ________ of

______ is like ________,

______ in a ____, that

a ____ ______ and

________. Then in ___

___ he _____ and _____

__________ he has

and _____ that _____."

________ ___:___-___

Word Bank

13	HEAVEN
44	HIS
45	JOY
BURIED	KINGDOM
BUYS	MAN
EVERYTHING	MATTHEW
FIELD (X 2)	REBURIED
FOUND	SELLS
GOES	TREASURE

Jesus often taught using parables, simple stories to teach a spiritual lesson. One day, Jesus shared a story of how heaven is like treasure. In Jesus' time period (around AD 30), they didn't have bank accounts to keep money like we do today. Instead, people buried their money or treasure for safe keeping where they could find it again when they needed it. This passage about hidden treasure says that when we find the true buried treasure of this life—a relationship with Jesus—it will compel us to do whatever it takes so we can obtain this treasure for ourselves. A relationship with Jesus and the gift of salvation is priceless. A relationship with Him is the true treasure we should seek to find.

For Kids...
What is the thing you love most (a toy, perhaps)? Now, think about selling that thing you love so much in order to have a relationship with Jesus.

For Grown Ups...
What would you have a hard time giving up? Would you be able to give up everything you have, just to have a relationship with God? This priceless gift of salvation is worth more than anything else in this world.

Solution on page 86

Help the Disciples Return to Jerusalem to Find Jesus in the Temple

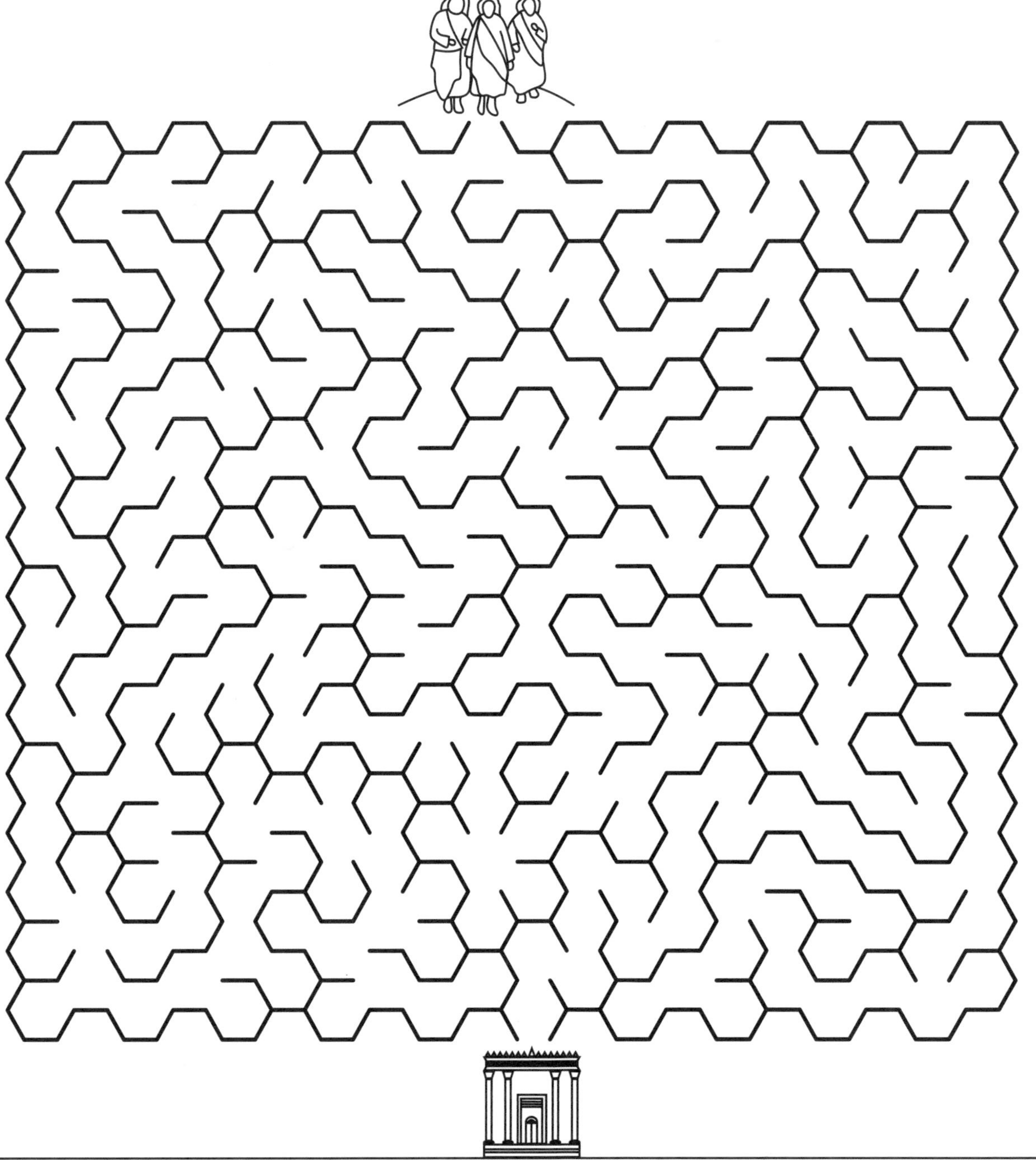

When they did not find [Jesus], they returned to Jerusalem to search for him. After three days, they found him in the temple sitting among the teachers, listening to them and asking them questions. (*Luke 2:45–46*)

Solution on page 87

Solve the Maze

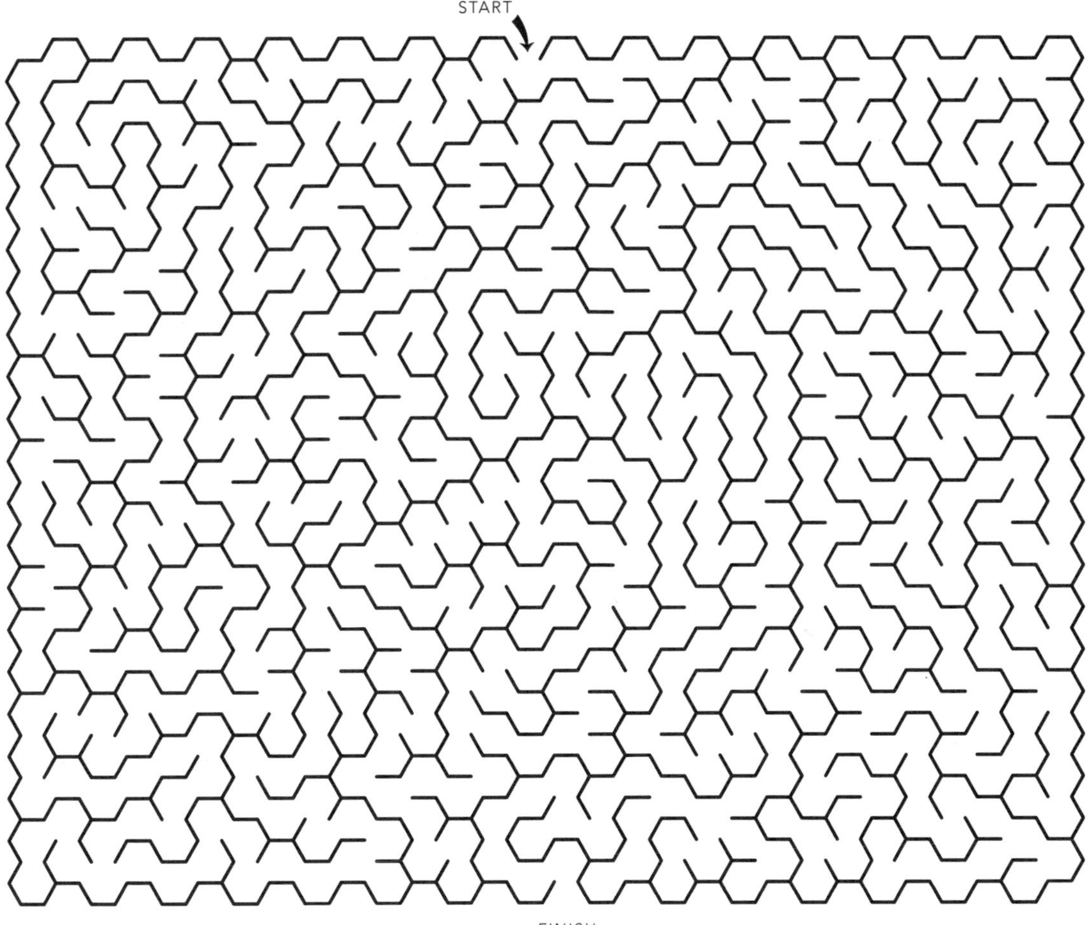

Mary and Joseph had traveled to Jerusalem for a Passover Festival with Jesus, but as they returned home, they noticed Jesus wasn't with them in their travelling party of family and friends. Jesus was lost! As you can imagine, they panicked and went the three-day journey back to Jerusalem. To their relief, they found Jesus sitting among teachers at the house of God, listening to them and asking them questions about God. Everyone was astounded that at the young age of twelve, Jesus had a depth of understanding about God that surpassed those much older than Him. While His parents were distraught about losing Him, Jesus felt no fear or concern because He was at His heavenly Father's house. Jesus had such a deep desire to pursue His heavenly Father, even at a young age. In the same way, let us not lose our desire to draw nearer to God and continue to invest in our relationship with Him.

For Kids...
What makes you feel closer to God? (i.e., singing to Him, reading/listening to stories about Him, sharing with others, praying, helping your parents or friends...) Keep doing these things so you can grow in your relationship with God!

For Grown Ups...
Do you desire God? How can you pursue Him more in your life and experience more of His presence?

Solution on page 87

How many can you find and color?

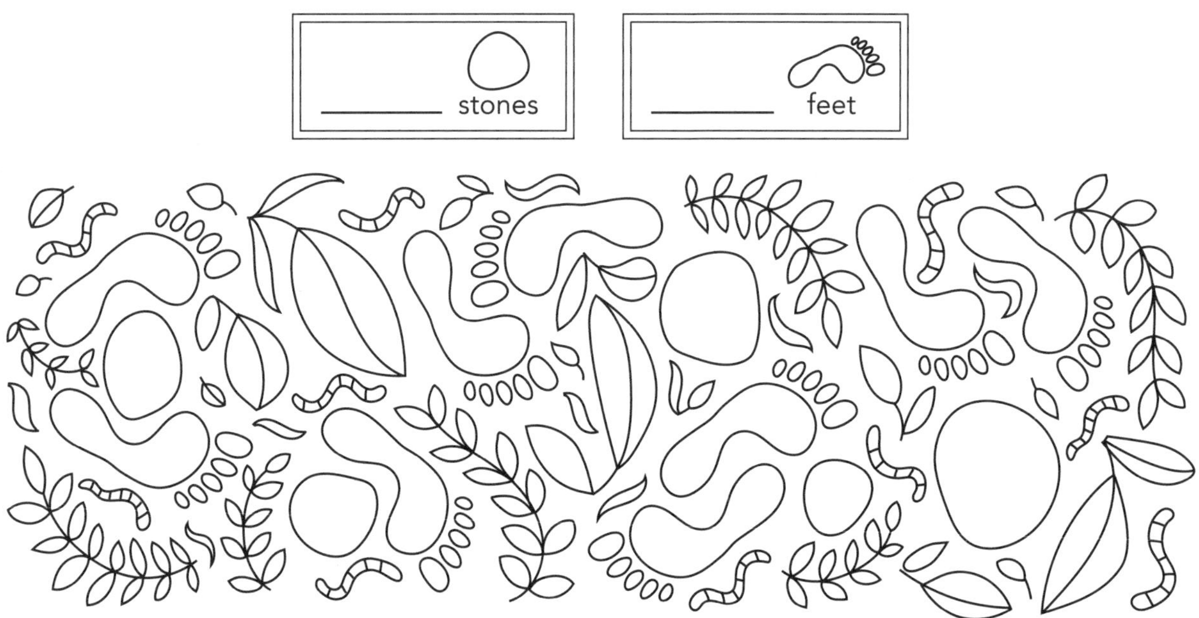

Use the ten frames to count how many pounds Goliath's armor weighed

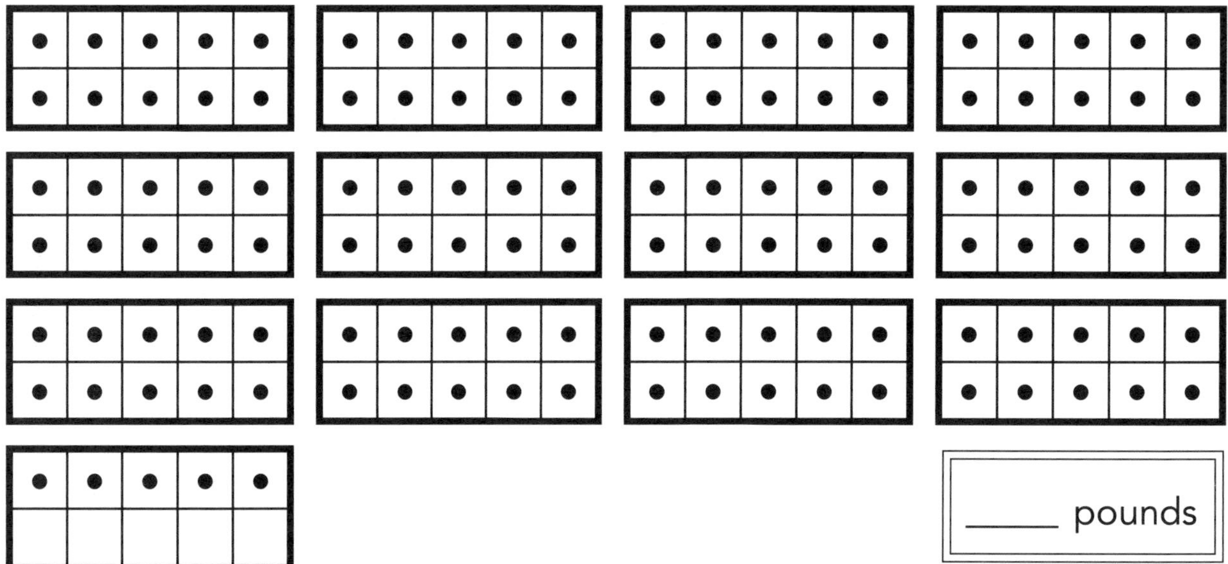

David said to the Philistine: "You come against me with a sword, spear, and javelin, but I come against you in the name of the LORD of Armies, the God of the ranks of Israel—you have defied him." (*1 Samuel 17:45)*

Solution on page 88

<table>
<tr><td></td><td></td><td>3</td><td></td><td>9</td><td></td><td>8</td><td></td><td></td></tr>
<tr><td>1</td><td></td><td>2</td><td>3</td><td></td><td></td><td></td><td></td><td>5</td></tr>
<tr><td>6</td><td>4</td><td></td><td></td><td></td><td></td><td></td><td></td><td></td></tr>
<tr><td></td><td>6</td><td></td><td></td><td>5</td><td>9</td><td></td><td>3</td><td></td></tr>
<tr><td>4</td><td></td><td>1</td><td></td><td></td><td></td><td>2</td><td></td><td>9</td></tr>
<tr><td></td><td>3</td><td></td><td>1</td><td>7</td><td></td><td></td><td>6</td><td></td></tr>
<tr><td></td><td></td><td></td><td></td><td></td><td></td><td></td><td>4</td><td>3</td></tr>
<tr><td>3</td><td></td><td></td><td></td><td></td><td>4</td><td>9</td><td></td><td>7</td></tr>
<tr><td></td><td></td><td>4</td><td></td><td>3</td><td></td><td>5</td><td></td><td></td></tr>
</table>

The Philistines were a group of people coming to attack the Israelites (God's chosen people). The Philistines had a giant champion named Goliath who was more than nine feet tall and wore full armor weighing over one-hundred and twenty-five pounds. Goliath asked if any man from the Israelite army wanted to fight. All the Israelites were afraid of Goliath, except one. A young man named David—small in stature and a simple sheepherder—believed that God would help him slay this giant. He took five small stones and his sling and ran forward to meet this giant in battle. With one shot, David killed Goliath and saved the Israelites. David believed that with God by his side, he had nothing to fear and that God would help him overcome this giant in his life.

For Kids...

What "giants" are you facing in your life right now? (i.e., school work, bully, fear) What step, knowing God is by your side, will you take to overcome this "giant"?

For Grown Ups...

We all have many "giants" we face in life. (i.e., fear, anger, disappointment, failure, rejection). What area of your life right now requires courage and trust in God, believing He will help you overcome the "giant" in front of you?

Solution on page 88

Follow the Steps to Draw the Father Welcoming the Son Home

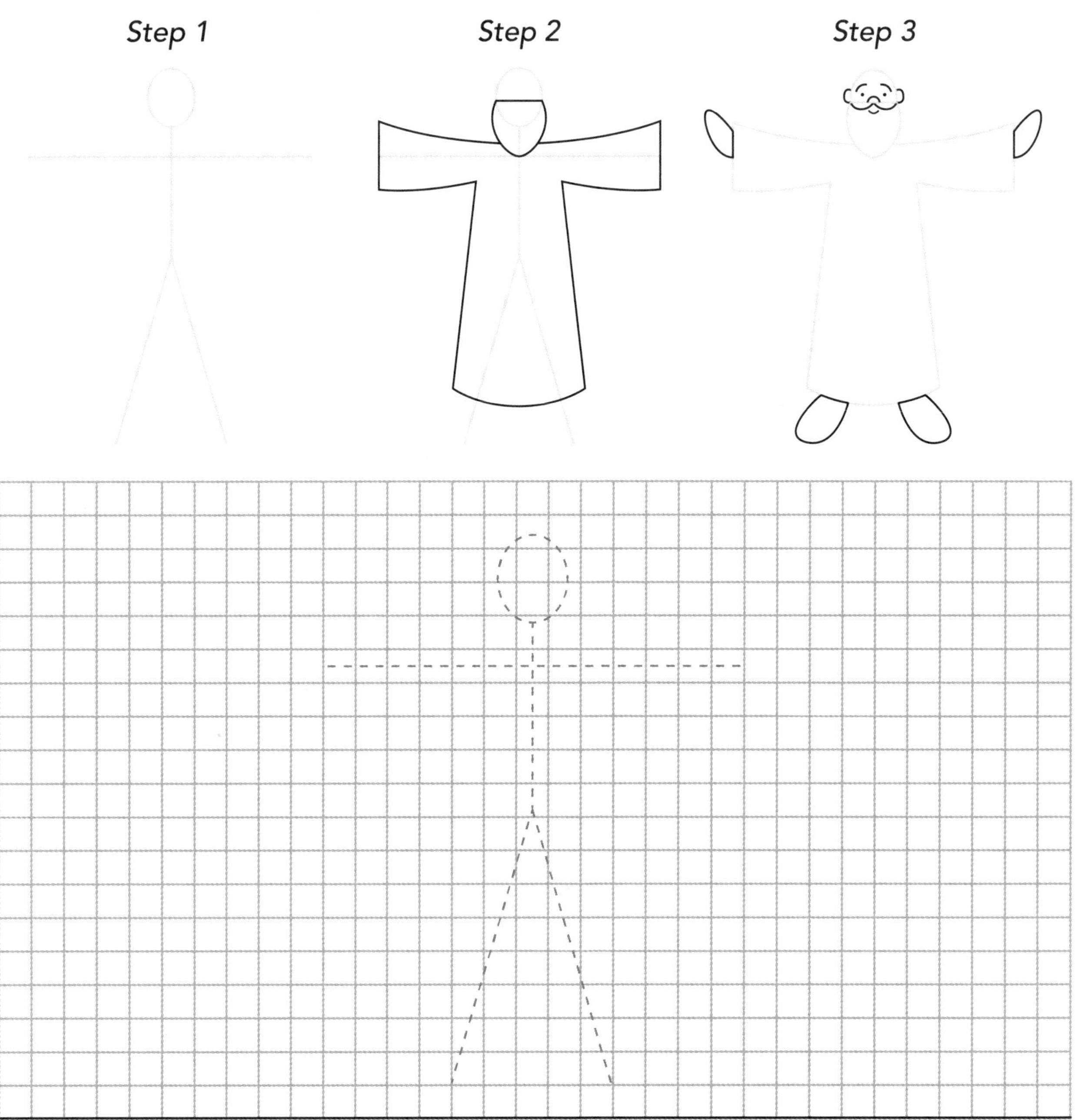

I'll get up, go to my father, and say to him, "Father, I have sinned against heaven and in your sight..." So he got up and went to his father. But while the son was still a long way off, his father saw him and was filled with compassion. He ran, threw his arms around his neck, and kissed him. (*Luke 15:18, 20)*

Follow the Steps to Draw the Father Welcoming the Son Home

Jesus once shared a story about a father who had two sons, but one went astray. This son took his inheritance money and squandered it with foolish living. It got even worse when a famine hit the land. With nothing but a rumbling belly, he decided to face his sin and shame by returning to his father, asking if he could work for him as a servant for food. As he returned home, his father saw him from a distance and ran to meet him. He embraced his son with compassion and love, instead of shame and bitterness. This prodigal son didn't feel worthy to be welcomed in this way, but his father insisted on celebrating his homecoming, forgiving him and demonstrating unconditional love. In the same way, God, our Father in Heaven, will always accept us back into His loving arms, forgiving us when we go astray.

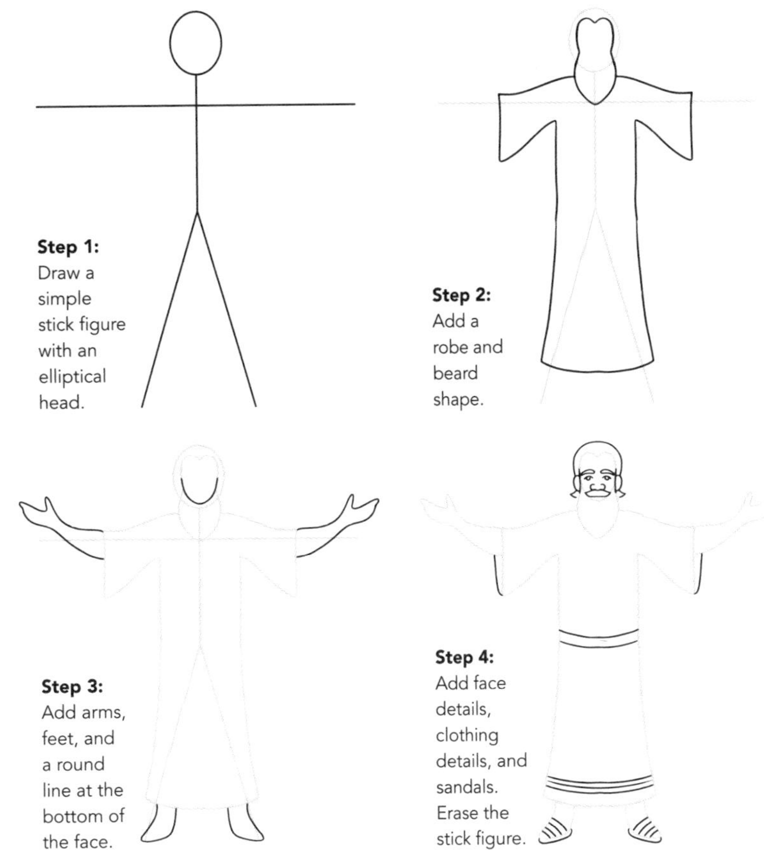

For Kids...
How does the father in this story compare to our Father in heaven? How does this make you feel?

For Grown Ups...
Did you know that no matter what you've done, God will always forgive you and accept you when you admit your failures and surrender to His love? Picture in your mind your heavenly Father running to you with open arms, welcoming you into His heavenly kingdom and celebrating your return to Him.

1 Corinthians 12:12 Crossword

Read the verses at the bottom of the page for clues.

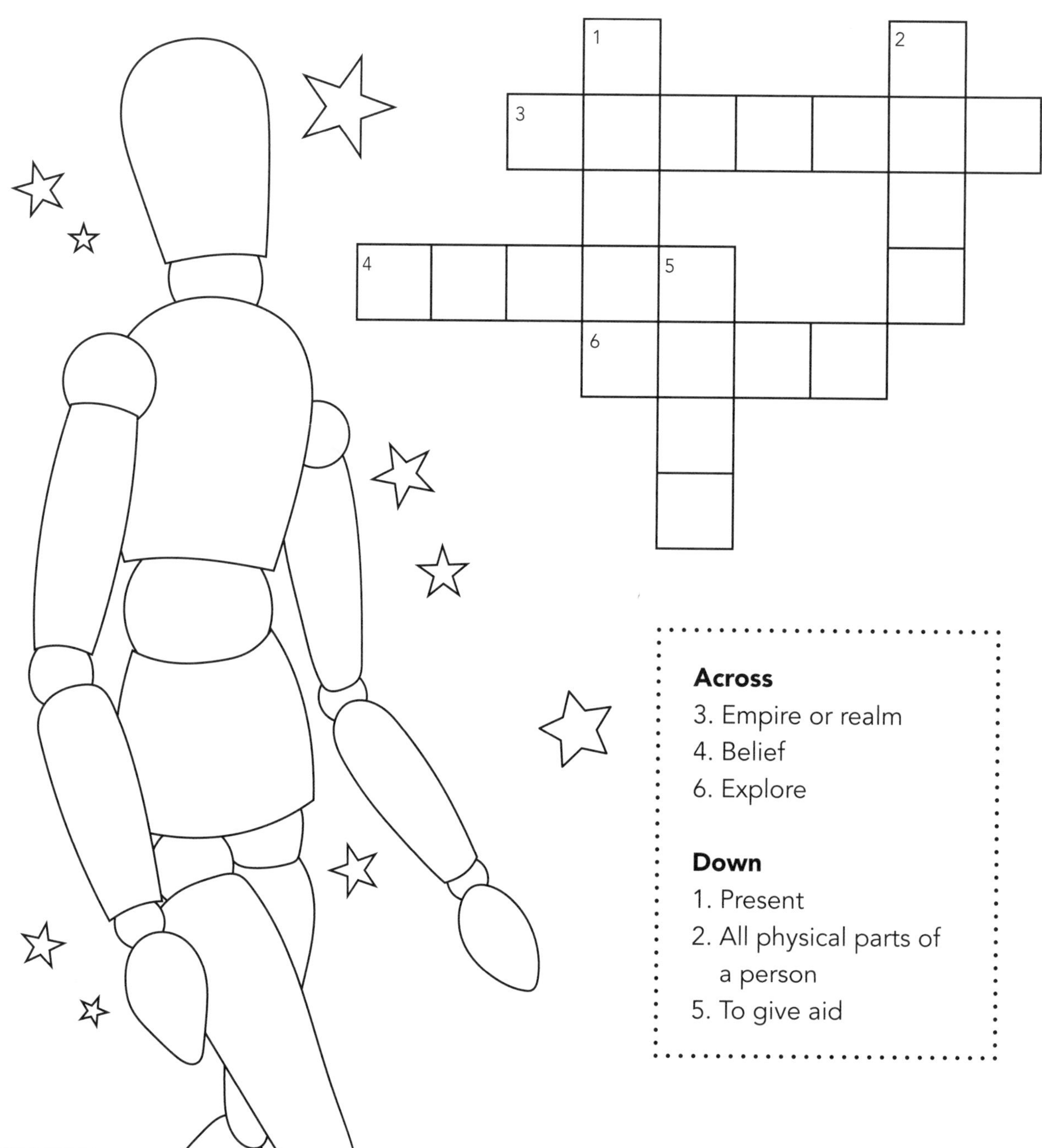

Across
3. Empire or realm
4. Belief
6. Explore

Down
1. Present
2. All physical parts of a person
5. To give aid

For just as the body is one and has many parts, and all the parts of that body, though many, are one body—so also is Christ. (*1 Corinthians 12:12*)

Solution on page 88

1 Corinthians 12 Crossword

Across

1. Compassion or forgiveness shown toward someone
4. Ability to judge between right and wrong
5. The end of the arm
7. Deep affection
9. Trust in God beyond human capability
10. To, for, or by every one of a group
11. Facts, information, and skills acquired by a person
12. Handing something over freely
14. Steer tasks and stay organized
16. Structure of a person
17. Whole
20. Pieces or segments of something
21. The body of knowledge and principles to make sound actions or decisions
22. Tend or look out for the spiritual welfare of others
24. Strong feeling of wanting something
25. Ability to make strangers and guests feel at ease

Down

2. Gifting to motivate and encourage someone to do something
3. Act of helpful activity
6. To become visible
7. Ability to direct others to accomplish goals
8. Enthusiastically lead others to Christ
13. Opposite of restrained
14. Gifting of those sent out on mission by Christ
15. Instructing others in truth
18. Numerous
19. Proclaiming boldly the truth from God
23. Belonging to a group
25. Make it easier for someone

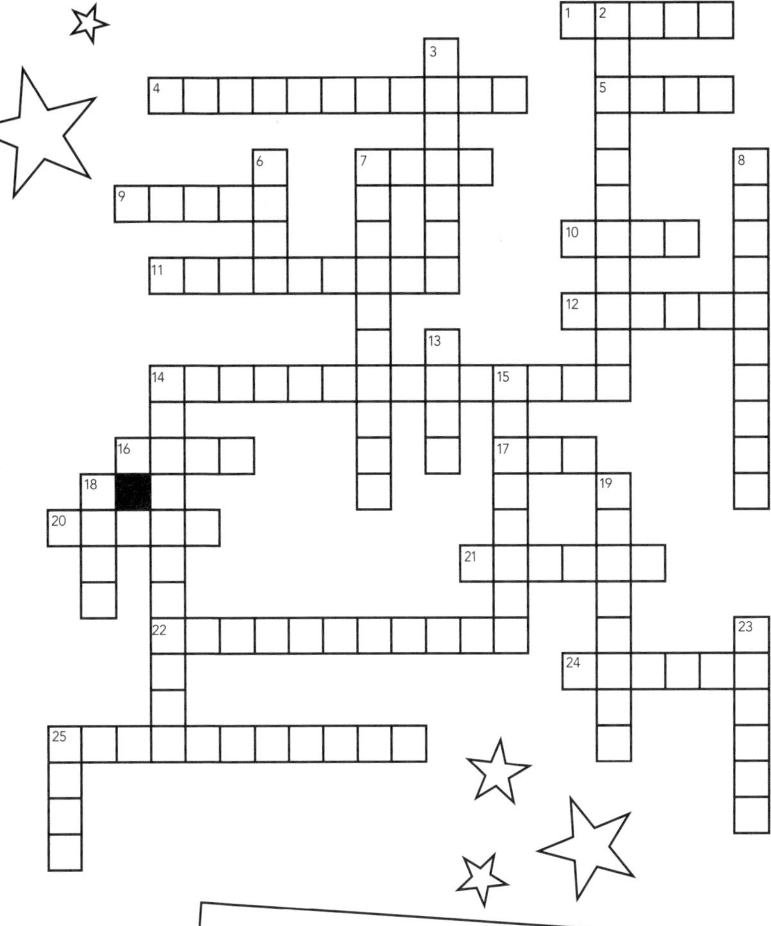

In 1 Corinthians 12, the apostle Paul writes about using our spiritual gifts and how we are all a part of the spiritual body of Christ. God gave us the Holy Spirit, which enables us to use our natural spiritual gifts that He's given to us to be used in amazing ways. He goes on to discuss how one person may have the gift of faith, another may have wisdom to share, another to heal, and so on. We each have a unique part to play in the spiritual body of Christ. If you're an eye, then you play a key role in the body to help it see. If you're a hand, then you use that hand to help the rest of the body. In the same way, we are to use our gifts as a body of believers, with the unique gifts we've been given, to help move forward God's kingdom, bringing God glory here on Earth. Through this, our spirits come alive with Christ as His Spirit moves in and through us to be used for a specific purpose in this world.

For Kids...

Have you explored your spiritual gifts? Think about what you love doing and how you can use that to help and serve others?

For Grown Ups...

Have you ever explored your spiritual gifts? Start exploring them! Sign up to serve at your church or take inventory of what you feel drawn to. (i.e., prayer, worship, organizing?) You have a unique role to play in this world. (Complete this free assessment to discover your spiritual gifts: https://www.lifeway.com/en/articles/women-leadership-spiritual-gifts-growth-service)

Solution on page 89

Match Each Item to Its Temperature

I know your works, that you are neither cold nor hot. I wish that you were cold or hot. So, because you are lukewarm, and neither hot nor cold, I am going to vomit you out of my mouth. (*Revelation 3:15–16*)

Trace and Color the Hot and Cold Items

There was a church called Laodicea (lay-o-dee-see-uh). It was filled with people who became lukewarm in their faith—neither hot nor cold, which is distasteful to God. After all, no one likes soup that is only kind of warm. They were distracted by their wealth and glorified themselves with material possessions. This inhibited their faith and desire for God. They were encouraged to repent and turn their hearts back to God to activate their faith wholly instead of settling with complacency. Have you seen other Christians and churches become distracted by wealth or other things that make them complacent in their desire to serve God? Maybe you're feeling this way right now? Remember, God loves a repentant heart and desires to use you in incredible ways to do amazing things for His glory, not for your glory.

For Kids...

One way to overcome the selfish desires of our hearts is to be an active giver. What can you give away this week to help someone else or bring glory to God through your generosity?

For Grown Ups...

One way to avoid becoming stagnant and lukewarm in your faith is to become an active and thankful giver. This week, pray and ask God to help you become more active in your faith by looking out for the needs of others and taking action to help others in need.

Page 1

Page 2

Page 3

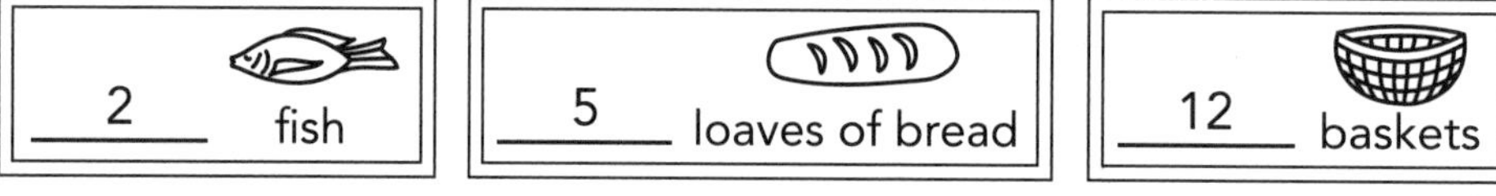

Page 4

8	3	4	6	7	2	5	9	1
7	9	6	3	1	5	8	2	4
2	1	5	8	9	4	7	6	3
3	8	9	2	6	1	4	5	7
6	5	1	7	4	3	9	8	2
4	2	7	9	5	8	1	3	6
5	4	3	1	2	9	6	7	8
9	6	2	4	8	7	3	1	5
1	7	8	5	3	6	2	4	9

Page 5

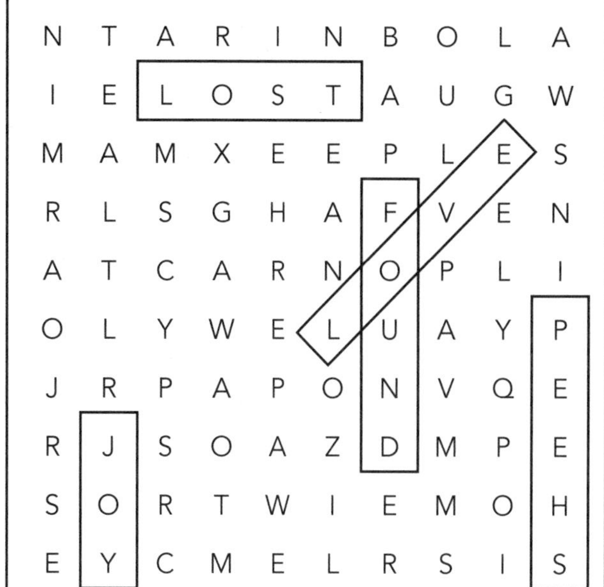

Page 6

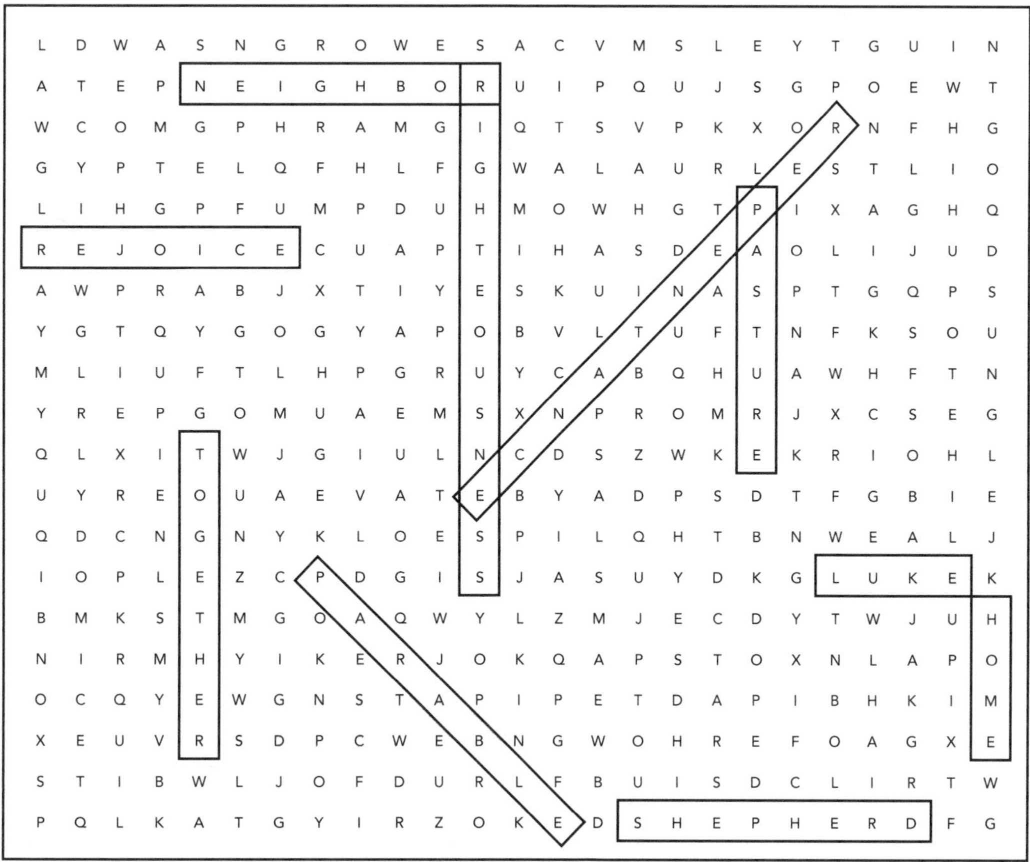

Page 13

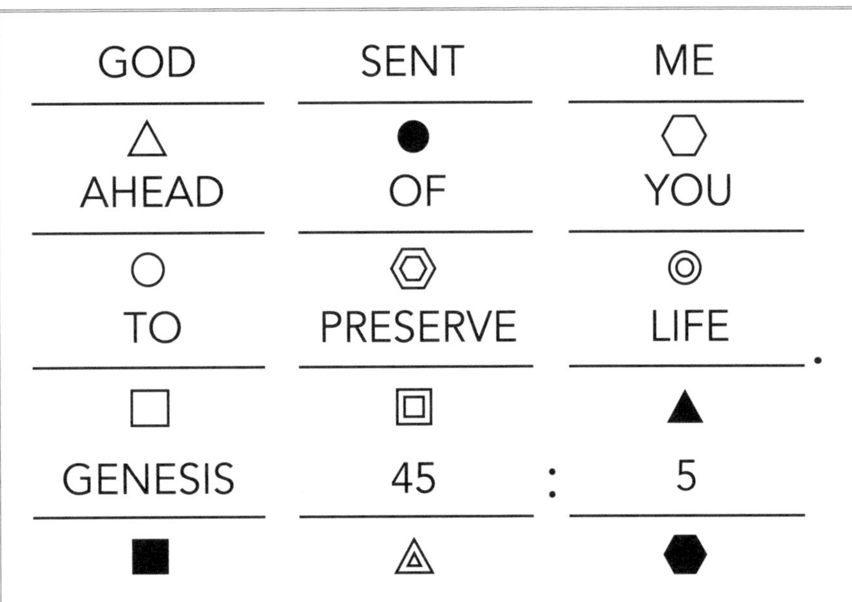

Page 14

A	B	C	D	E	F	G	H	I	J	K	L	M	N	O	P	Q	R	S	T	U	V	W	X	Y	Z
23	22	1	10	6	12	5	8	13	9	14	21	11	20	16	18	15	3	4	19	24	26	2	17	7	25

I		A	M		J	O	S	E	P	H		Y	O	U	R		B	R	O	T	H	E	R		H	E
13		23	11		9	16	4	6	18	8		7	16	24	3		22	3	16	19	8	6	3		8	6

S	A	I	D		T	H	E		O	N	E		Y	O	U		S	O	L	D		I	N	T	O
4	23	13	10		19	8	6		16	20	6		7	16	24		4	16	21	10		13	20	19	16

E	G	Y	P	T		A	N	D		N	O	W		D	O	N	T		B	E		G	R	I	E	V	E	D
6	5	7	18	19		23	20	10		20	16	2		10	16	20	19		22	6		5	3	13	6	16	6	10

O	R		A	N	G	R	Y		W	I	T	H		Y	O	U	R	S	E	L	V	E	S		F	O	R
16	3		23	20	5	3	7		2	13	19	8		7	16	24	3	4	6	21	26	6	4		12	16	3

S	E	L	L	I	N	G		M	E		H	E	R	E		B	E	C	A	U	S	E		G	O	D
4	6	21	21	13	20	5		11	6		8	6	3	6		22	6	25	23	24	4	6		5	16	10

S	E	N	T		M	E		A	H	E	A	D		O	F		Y	O	U		T	O
4	6	20	19		11	6		23	8	6	23	10		16	12		7	16	24		19	16

P	R	E	S	E	R	V	E		L	I	F	E		G	E	N	E	S	I	S
18	3	6	4	6	3	26	6		21	13	12	6		5	6	20	6	4	13	4

4 5 : 4 - 5

Page 17

Page 18

Page 19

Page 20

Page 21 *Page 22*

Page 25

LOVE
HEART
SOUL
STRENGTH
MIND
NEIGHBOR
YOURSELF
MARK

Page 26

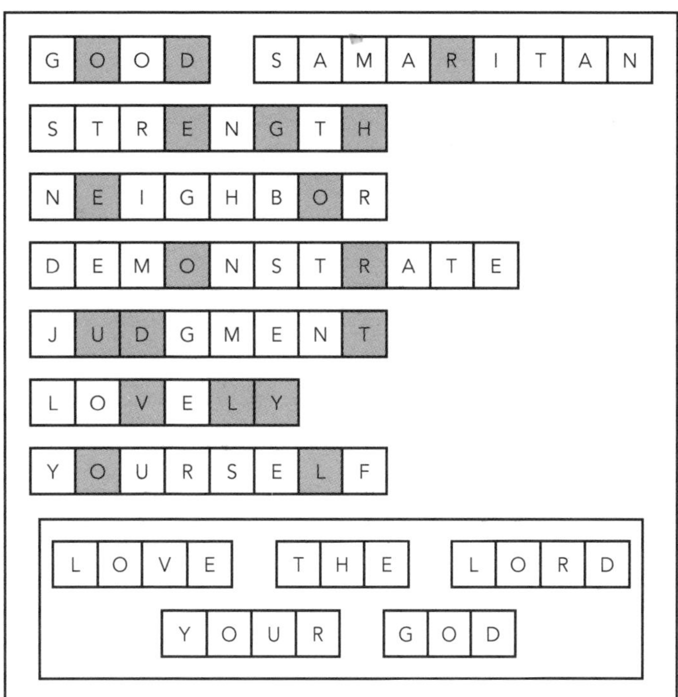

Page 33

Page 34

Page 37

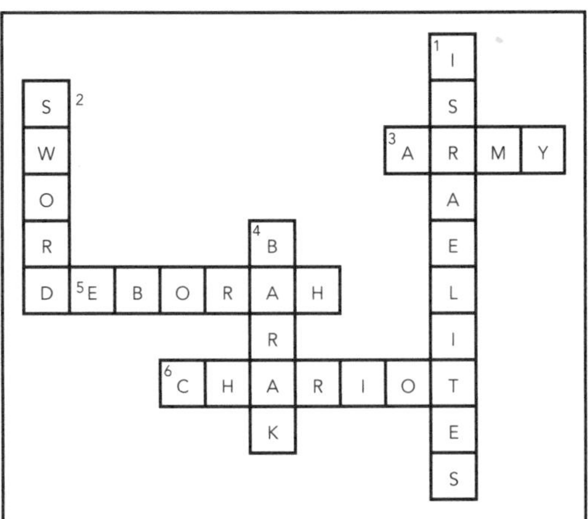

Page 38

1 DISPUTES (across)
2 SUMMONED (down)
3 EPHRAIM (across)
4 PALM (down)
5 ZEBULUN (across)
5 ZAANANNIM (down)
6 DEPLOY (across)
7 PEACE (across)
8 LORD (across)
8 LAPPIDOTH (down)
9 INFANTRY (down)
10 PANIC (across)
11 IRON (across)
12 PEG (across)
13 POWER (down)
14 JAEL (down)
15 COMMANDER (across)
16 BLANKET (across)
16 BARAK (down)
17 INCREASE (down)
18 SINGLE (across)
18 SISERA (down)
19 TABOR (across)
20 WATER (down)
21 TENT (across)
22 HEBER (across)
22 HONOR (down)

Page 39

Page 40

A	B	C	D	E	F	G	H	I	J	K	L	M	N	O	P	Q	R	S	T	U	V	W	X	Y	Z
10	23	16	8	17	26	14	7	11	5	12	18	24	13	22	15	4	21	2	9	1	25	3	19	20	6

N	E	V	E	R	T	H	E	L	E	S	S	,	I		A	M		T	E	L	L	I	N	G		Y	O	U
13	17	25	17	21	9	7	17	18	17	2	2		11		10	24		9	17	18	18	11	13	14		20	22	1

T	H	E		T	R	U	T	H	.	I	T		I	S		F	O	R		Y	O	U	R
9	7	17		9	21	1	9	7		11	9		11	2		26	22	21		20	22	1	21

B	E	N	E	F	I	T		T	H	A	T		I		G	O		A	W	A	Y	,
23	17	13	17	26	11	9		9	7	10	9		11		14	22		10	3	10	20	

B	E	C	A	U	S	E		I	F		I		D	O	N	T		G	O		A	W	A	Y		T	H	E
23	17	16	10	1	2	17		11	26		11		8	22	13	9		14	22		10	3	10	20		9	7	17

C	O	U	N	S	E	L	O	R		W	I	L	L		N	O	T		C	O	M	E		T	O
16	22	1	13	2	17	18	22	21		3	11	18	18		13	22	9		16	22	24	17		9	22

Y	O	U	.	I	F		I		G	O	,	I		W	I	L	L		S	E	N	D		H	I	M
20	22	1		11	26		11		14	22		11		3	11	18	18		2	17	13	8		7	11	24

T	O		Y	O	U		J	O	H	N		1	6	:	7
9	22		20	22	1		5	22	7	13					

Page 41

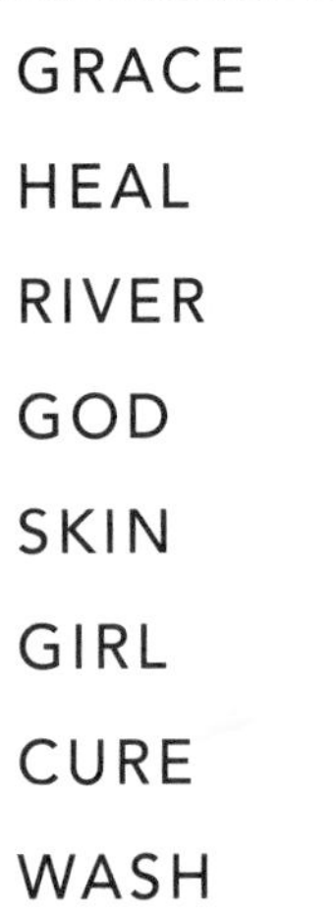

Page 42

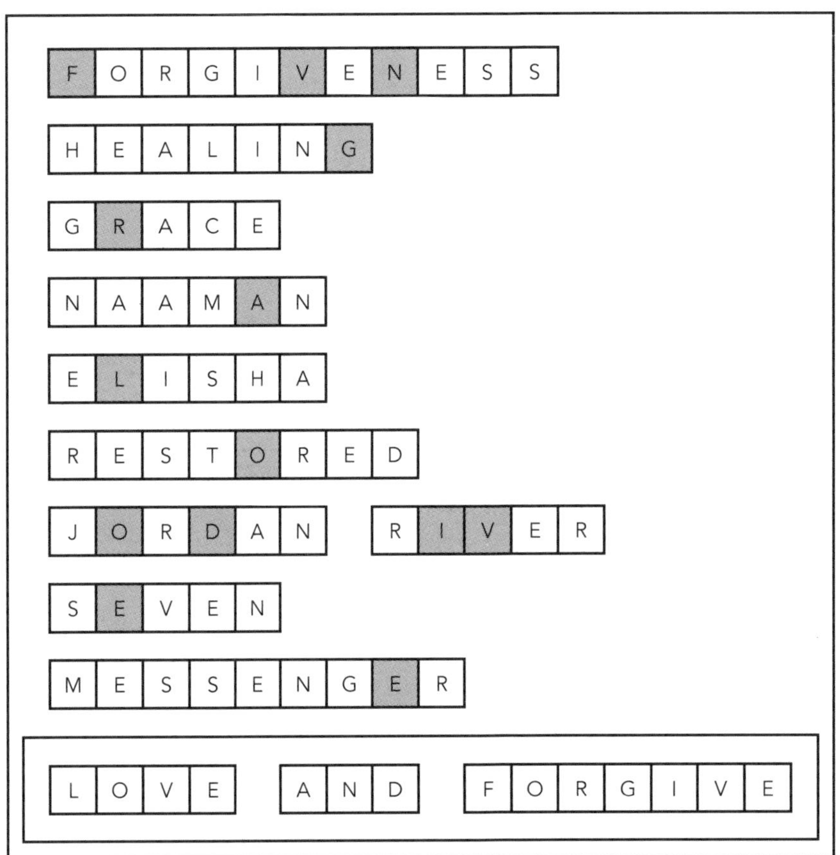

Page 45

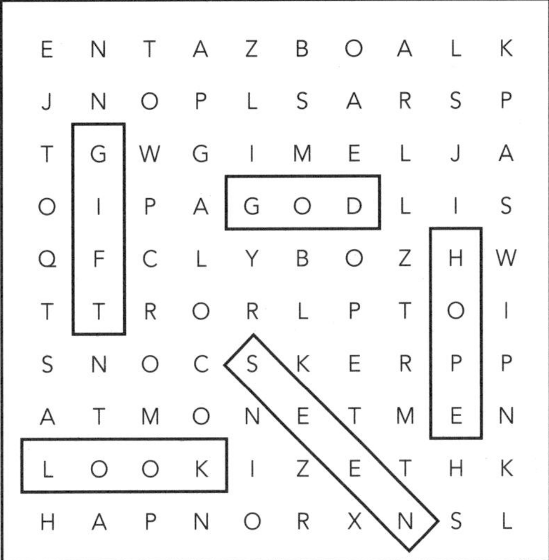

Page 46

L	D	W	A	S	N	G	T	O	W	E	S	A	C	V	M	S	S	E	Y	T	G	U	I	N
A	T	E	P	N	E	C	H	E	R	I	S	H	E	D	Q	P	J	S	G	P	O	E	W	T
W	C	O	M	G	P	H	R	A	M	G	I	Q	T	S	E	P	K	R	O	R	N	S	H	G
G	Y	P	T	E	L	Q	O	H	L	F	G	W	A	C	A	U	R	E	E	S	T	I	I	O
L	I	H	G	P	F	U	U	P	D	U	H	M	I	W	H	G	T	M	I	X	A	G	H	Q
D	E	J	O	I	C	E	G	U	A	P	T	A	H	A	S	D	E	I	O	L	I	N	U	D
E	W	P	R	A	B	J	H	L	I	Y	L	S	K	U	I	N	A	N	P	T	G	I	P	S
S	G	T	Q	Y	G	O	G	E	A	P	O	B	V	L	T	U	F	D	N	F	K	F	O	U
I	L	I	U	F	T	L	H	A	G	V	U	Y	C	A	B	Q	H	E	A	W	H	I	T	N
R	R	E	P	G	O	M	U	H	E	M	I	X	N	P	R	O	M	R	J	X	C	C	E	G
E	L	X	I	T	W	J	G	I	U	L	N	S	D	S	Z	W	K	S	K	R	I	A	H	L
D	Y	R	E	O	U	A	E	V	A	T	E	B	H	A	D	P	S	D	T	F	G	N	I	E
O	P	E	N	E	D	Y	K	L	O	E	S	P	G	E	N	E	S	I	S	W	E	T	L	J
I	O	P	L	E	Z	C	P	D	G	I	S	J	A	S	D	Y	D	K	G	A	O	X	T	K
B	M	K	S	T	M	G	O	A	Q	W	Y	L	Z	M	J	E	C	D	Y	T	W	J	U	H
N	I	R	M	T	A	L	E	N	T	S	O	K	Q	A	E	S	T	O	X	N	L	A	P	O
O	C	Q	Y	E	W	G	N	S	T	A	P	I	P	E	F	D	A	P	I	B	H	K	I	M
X	E	U	V	R	S	D	P	C	W	E	B	N	G	W	I	H	R	E	F	O	A	G	X	E
S	T	I	B	W	L	J	O	F	D	U	R	L	F	E	L	T	S	D	C	L	I	R	T	W
P	Q	L	K	A	T	G	Y	I	R	Z	O	K	A	Q	Y	T	E	P	H	E	R	D	F	G

Page 53

N	T	A	R	I	N	B	O	L	A
I	E	L	O	J	T	A	U	G	W
M	S	T	R	O	N	G	L	E	S
P	L	S	G	Y	A	F	V	E	N
A	T	C	A	F	N	O	P	L	I
T	L	K	W	U	L	U	A	Y	P
I	R	P	I	L	O	V	E	L	Y
E	J	S	O	N	Z	D	M	P	E
N	O	R	T	W	D	E	M	O	H
T	Y	C	M	E	L	R	S	I	S

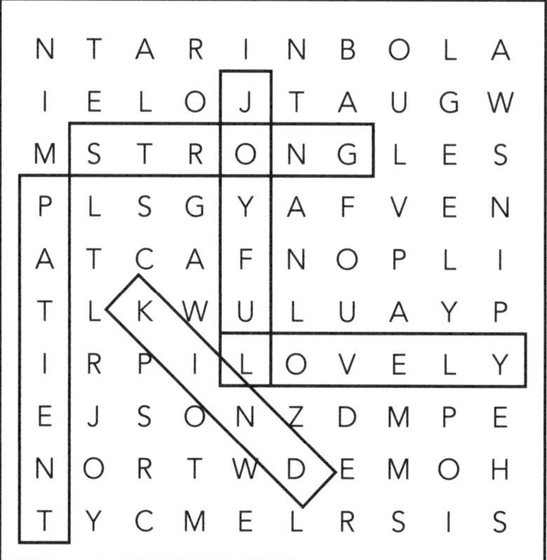

Page 54

L	D	W	A	S	B	G	K	O	W	E	S	A	C	V	M	A	R	V	E	L	O	U	S	S
A	T	E	C	H	E	R	I	S	H	E	D	U	I	P	Q	U	J	S	G	P	O	E	W	T
W	C	O	M	G	L	H	R	A	M	G	I	Q	T	F	V	P	K	X	O	R	N	F	H	G
G	Y	P	T	E	O	Q	F	H	L	F	R	E	M	A	R	K	A	B	L	E	T	L	I	O
L	I	H	G	P	V	U	M	P	D	U	H	M	O	I	H	G	T	E	I	X	A	G	H	Q
B	E	J	T	H	E	E	C	U	A	P	T	I	H	T	S	T	R	O	N	G	L	J	U	D
A	W	P	R	A	D	J	X	T	C	Y	E	S	K	H	I	N	A	S	P	T	G	Q	P	S
Y	G	T	Q	Y	H	O	G	Y	R	P	O	B	V	F	T	U	F	T	N	F	K	S	O	U
M	L	I	U	F	T	W	I	S	E	R	M	Y	C	U	B	Q	H	Y	A	W	H	F	T	N
Y	R	E	P	G	O	M	U	A	A	M	S	X	S	L	R	O	M	R	J	X	C	S	E	G
Q	L	X	I	K	W	J	D	I	T	L	N	C	O	S	Z	W	K	V	K	R	I	O	H	A
U	Y	R	E	O	U	E	E	V	E	T	T	V	Y	A	D	P	S	D	T	F	G	B	I	M
Q	D	C	J	N	S	Y	K	L	D	E	E	P	I	L	Q	A	T	B	N	K	I	N	D	A
I	O	P	L	O	Z	C	O	D	G	L	S	J	A	S	U	T	D	K	G	L	R	K	E	Z
B	M	K	P	N	Y	G	O	A	Y	W	Y	L	Z	M	J	I	C	D	Y	T	W	J	U	I
N	I	R	M	H	Y	F	Z	E	R	J	O	K	Q	A	P	E	T	O	X	N	L	A	P	N
O	U	Q	Y	E	W	G	U	S	T	D	P	I	P	E	T	N	A	P	I	B	H	K	I	G
P	E	U	V	R	S	D	P	L	W	E	B	N	G	W	O	T	R	E	F	O	A	G	X	E
S	T	I	B	W	L	J	O	F	D	U	R	L	F	B	U	H	S	D	C	L	I	R	T	W
P	Q	L	K	A	T	G	Y	I	R	Z	O	K	E	D	S	P	E	L	H	Q	R	D	F	G

Page 57

Page 59

GIRL

AFRAID

BELIEVE

JESUS

LEADER

SAVED

LUKE

Page 60

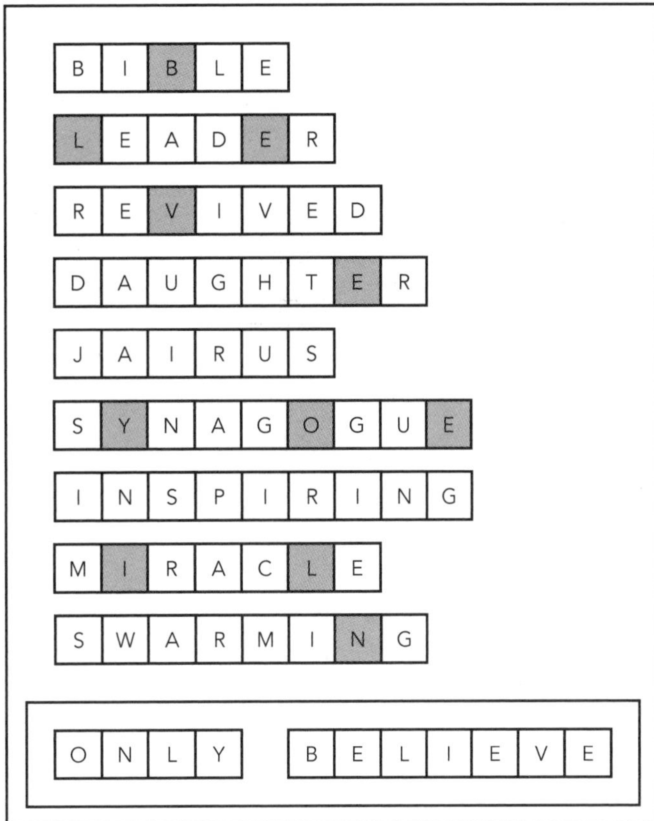

Page 61

The **kingdom** of **heaven** is like **treasure**

Page 62

"The **kingdom** of **heaven** is like **treasure**, **buried** in a **field**, that a **man** **found** and **reburied**. Then in **his joy** he **goes** and **sells everything** he has and **buys** that **field**."

Matthew 13:44-45

Page 63

Page 64

Page 65

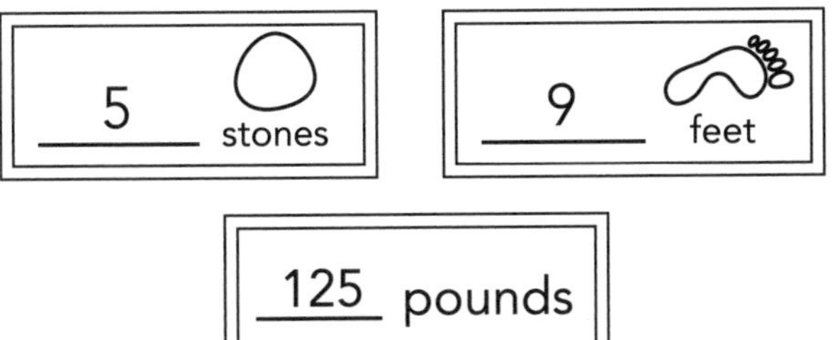

Page 66

7	**5**	3	**2**	9	**6**	8	**1**	**4**
1	**8**	2	3	**4**	**7**	**6**	**9**	5
6	4	**9**	**8**	**1**	**5**	**3**	**7**	**2**
2	6	**8**	**4**	5	9	**7**	3	**1**
4	**7**	1	**6**	**8**	**3**	2	**5**	9
9	3	**5**	1	7	**2**	**4**	6	**8**
5	**2**	**7**	**9**	**6**	**8**	**1**	4	3
3	**1**	**6**	**5**	**2**	4	9	**8**	7
8	**9**	4	**7**	3	**1**	5	**2**	**6**

Page 69

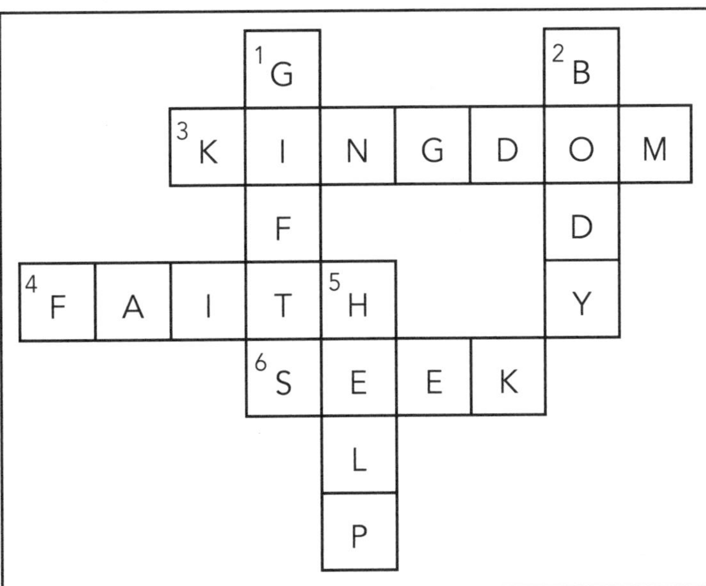

Page 70

MERCY
EXHORTATION
SERVICE
DISCERNMENT
HAND
SHO
LOVE
LEADERSHIP
EVANGELISM
FAITH
TEACH
KNOWLEDGE
GIVING
FREE
ADMINISTRATION
TEACHING
APOSTLESHIP
BODY
ALL
MANY
PROPHECY
PARTS
WISDOM
SHEPHERDING
MEMBER
DESIRE
HOSPITALITY
HELP

About the Author and Illustrator

Rachel Swanson is a best-selling and multiple award-winning author, inspirational speaker, podcaster, and accredited Christian life coach. She's the author of *Refine and Restore* and *Big and Little Coloring Devotional*. After she and her husband wrangle their Wannabe Triplets off to school in the mornings, she enjoys sipping her chai lattes on her rustic patio admiring the rural hills of southern Idaho. Find out more about her and her faith-filled adventures at RachelCSwanson.com.

Jacy Corral (pronounced "Jackie") is an illustrator, hand lettering artist, and graphic designer - plus a wife and mom. After enjoying an extensive career in corporate marketing and design, she traded fancy slacks for yoga pants to focus on the great privilege of raising her kids, investing in her home and marriage, and creating artwork that helps people to connect and reflect through beautiful design. Jacy lives with her husband, children, and miniature poodle in Los Angeles, California. She shares her creations regularly on Instagram and at www.jacycorral.com.

ALSO AVAILABLE